VERTICALS | writings

MuseumsEtc

Photography and the Artist's Book

Essays by

Sarah Bodman, Sylvia Grace Borda, Tim Daly, Lawrence George Giles, Angela Kelly, Adam Murray, Elisabeth Neudörfl, Jane Pendlebury, David Penny, Jane Simon, Logan Sisley, Diane Smyth, Adam Paul Verity and Theresa Wilkie.

Edited by

Theresa Wilkie, Jonathan Carson and Rosie Miller

MuseumsEtc
Edinburgh and Boston

Contents

PRACTICE

Editors' acknowledgements

Our thanks go to the authors of each of the chapters presented here.

In addition we would to thank all the staff at Manchester Metropolitan University Special Collections, particularly Stephanie Boydell, Jeremy Parrett and Jane Pendlebury, also Gill Barry, Head of Library Services at Manchester Metropolitan University, and Jayne Burgess, Library Services Manager (Art and Design), for supporting the project.

Foreword

Photography and the Artist's Book is a welcome addition to the bibliography of artists' books. It ranges from nineteenth-century photographic books to contemporary artists' book practice, examining an aspect of artists' books that is currently of high interest but that has endured since the beginning of the modern artists' book. Certain issues and values emerge from *Photography and the Artist's Book*. The democratic impulse, the desire for dissemination and access are key values shared by artists and librarians. The nature of the book, its structure and sequence, its physical reality, is referenced and examined by both commentators and practitioners. Recurring themes can be identified, including appropriation, the use of found images and the referencing of other works.

Tate Library has a collection of approximately 5,500 artists' books dating from the 1960s onwards. Like Manchester Metropolitan University Special Collections, the collection is international in scope, with an emphasis on British artists. The collection, which actively acquires, contains many works which explore or use photography or found photographs. These include books by Frans Baake, Sarah Bodman, Christian Boltanski, Tacita Dean, Helen Douglas,

Hans-Peter Feldmann, Hamish Fulton, Richard Long, Martin Parr, Ed Ruscha, Telfer Stokes, Fiona Tan and Tom Sowden, all of whom are discussed in *Photography and the Artist's Book*. Perhaps it is relevant that Ed Ruscha's *Twentysix gasoline stations*, which is credited by some as being the first modern artists' book, dated 1962 but published in April 1963, is a *photographic* record of petrol stations along the highway from Los Angeles to Oklahoma City (but not in geographical sequence).[1] Photography has been employed to lead the reader through themes such as memory, land, nature, journey, movement, loss, death, portraiture and self-portraiture. Works have fabricated, appropriated, documented, used research from archives, and embodied exhibitions and performances. The variety of photographic artists' books is great indeed.

This volume, with its examination of content and practice, and the symposium that preceded it, reflect upon a moment in the history of artists' books and their interaction with photography, and plays a part in that history.

Maria White
Tate Library
London

NOTES

1 Clive Phillpot, Twentysix gasoline stations that shook the world: the rise and fall of cheap booklets as art, *Art Libraries Journal*, Vol. 18, No. 1 (1993), p. 6.

Introduction

There is a renewed interest in the relationship of photography and the artist's book as an art form and as an alternative site for exhibition and dissemination. There is also a notable expansion in the activities of self-publication by photographers and artists who use the photograph. This book has been developed from a day-long symposium which explored these issues. The response to the call for papers for the symposium, and the breadth of engagement which was experienced within the day itself, demonstrated a substantial level of interest and a range of connections to the subject matter that supports the publication of this book.

While the symposium explored some particular themes – the photographic essay and other narrative forms; sequence, seriality and typology; and the relationship between the audience for the form and the form itself – this book is divided into two sections: *Context* and *Practice*. These sections allow a fluid approach to considering the relationship between photography and the artist's book, encouraging the cross-referencing of issues, debates and forms of practice. Of course, when tackling an issue of this kind, the temptation to define the form is hard to resist but is equally difficult to contain. This is exemplified by the range of terms used across the chapters – *artist's book*, *artist's photographic book*, *photographic artist's book*, *photobook* – and is also considered by a number of contributors in some detail. These are valuable discussions that are pertinent to a form with a currency that sees it still positioned within contemporary creative practice and growing more complex in its production and subsequent categorisation. To reflect this, the book presents a range of approaches to the subject matter in order to provide texture to the debates, discussions and reflections included here. Predominantly visual chapters sit alongside entirely written texts – other chapters represent dialogues or correspondence between authors.

Our work as editors is framed by our work as practitioners who relate to photography and the artist's book in different ways. Our experiences of the photograph embrace both the making of images and the use of 'found' or existing photographs. We share an understanding of the production of the book and a concern with the space the book can provide an artist or photographer as a unique form through which to engage an audience. As such, these shared experiences offer a useful perspective on the subject and the texts presented here.

Context begins with Sylvia Grace Borda's chapter, *The Artist's Photographic Book: towards a definition*, which gives an important historical perspective to this book. Borda asks us – from a contemporary viewpoint – to review what the artist's book is, especially in relation to the use of images produced in the context of early photography. By examining what she and others speculate could be the earliest example of an artist's photographic book, Borda reveals that, even at this early stage of development, some of the key concerns of practitioners, such as Anna Atkins, are still key concerns almost 170 years later: how do images and text relate? How might this influence the layout of the book? How to publish the book? These concerns are echoed in a number of other chapters, for example in Adam Murray and Diane Smyth's correspondence, in Jane Simon's examination of Francesca Woodman's books and in David Penny's visual essay.

In *Locating Photography and the Artist's Book*, Theresa Wilkie and Jane Pendlebury examine these forms through a dialogue that explores a very particular collection. The Artists' Book collection at Manchester Metropolitan University Special

Collections offers a particular type of access to these books. One of the dichotomies of the artist's book lies in the maker's impulse to democratise circulation and the manner in which such books can become rarefied through the limited edition. At MMU Special Collections these polarities are cut through in that this is an open-shelf, browsable collection. Each book, regardless of perceived value, can be both deliberately searched for or stumbled upon. The collection offers far-reaching public access, coming close to what is, for many, a fundamental principle of the artist's book form: that it is something for us all. Wilkie and Pendlebury explore the collection and, in turn, access to and use of it, drawing on their perspectives as both collector and user. In their chapter, Murray and Smyth also reflect on MMU Special Collections, which they suggest might be a preferred means of experiencing artists' books, in comparison to book fairs or exhibitions.

Adam Paul Verity considers access and circulation in his chapter *Print/Screen: current and future dissemination of the self-published artist's book*. Inevitably, Verity reflects on technological developments and the complex relationship these developments have to the democratic impulse that Wilkie and Pendlebury consider in terms of a particular collection. For some practitioners the movement from the physical artefact to the digital raises new issues in terms of what might be framed as the 'future heritage' of these forms – how can they be protected and archived? A further dimension to the expansion of virtual forms is a shift in editioning practice which has been an important device for the tradition of the artist's book, and so Verity considers the implications of editioning in digital formats. In line with Angela Kelly's comments regarding the photographer in the digital age, Verity acknowledges the variable elements that technology brings to both the photograph and the book form.

In the chapter *Pictures of Things and Things That Are Pictures*, David Penny presents a visual essay; an example of artistic research and its document as artist's book. Here, thoughts and questions are presented both in relation to the creation of an artist's book and as a reflection on their creation. Via this contextualised view of practice Penny explores the relationship between the structure and sequencing of a book – its text and its images – and he also helps us to reflect on editing as an artistic impulse. In contrast, in *Photographs, Notebooks, Interiority: Francesca Woodman's artist's books*, Jane Simon reflects on Woodman's use of the pre-existing book that is then affected by the artist. Simon suggests that many readings of Woodman's work lead to an autobiographical interpretation. However, within her chapter, Simon breaks with this interpretation and focuses on Woodman's manipulation of the interior space and physicality of the book, the relationship between the photograph and the found book, and strategies of appropriation and layering evident within Woodman's bookworks.

Appropriation is also a theme considered by Logan Sisley in his chapter, *Artists' Interventions in the Family Album*. Here Sisley discusses the use of found or lost photographs and their re-use by a number of artists in a range of book projects. These artists re-work the notion of the family album by disrupting the traditional relationship between image and narrative and, as Sisley argues, open the photographs to new meanings and new contexts. In some cases the act of appropriation is, in itself, the artistic impulse and in others this appropriation is further affected by such methods of cropping, enlarging and re-sequencing. Sisley explores the difference between notions of the domestic and the everyday, especially in the work of Fiona Tan and Tacita Dean, where photographs (highly valued or discarded) are used to question the conventions of the family photograph and to put these images in tension with other interpretations that might come about through the reframing of the family album. In parallel to these explorations an undercurrent of the democratised image emerges. The album format offers these artists a familiar visual language which we can also observe in both Angela Kelly's chapter and Lawrence George Giles' visual essay, which reflect on the use of the family photograph and the conceit of the album.

The second section of this book, *Practice*, begins with Kelly's chapter *Book, Exhibition, Lecture, Website – revisiting Catharsis: Images of Post-Conflict Belfast*. Here, along with a number of other chapters, we have the privilege of gaining some insight into the considerations an artist makes when grappling with the early stages of developing a new artist's book. Kelly begins to negotiate the space of the book in relation to the space of the photograph. Like Simon's exploration of Woodman's work, Kelly examines the physicality of both book and photograph and how they might affect one another. She also – in a way that connects with some of Murray and Smyth's discussion – speculates on digital space and how this affects the relationship between photography and the book format. A further important consideration in Kelly's chapter is the family album. Like Sisley and Giles, Kelly taps into the rich vein of these pictorial commentaries of our lives tangling the past and present, the political and the personal, the intimate and the formal.

Where Kelly considers the development of a future artist's book in the context of her current practice, Elisabeth Neudörfl writes about her completed and published book *E.D.S.A* in her chapter *Space–Time–Fragment: conceptual documentary photography in the artist's book as a tool of analysis*. Neudörfl's focus is primarily on sequence as a methodology that is well suited to both the behaviour of the camera and the book format. Referencing the seminal works of Robert Frank and Ed Ruscha, Neudörfl carefully considers mapping, narrative and arrangement, paying particular attention to this in the editorial process. The images of *E.D.S.A.* mimic their subject matter. They stream through the book in an allusion to the thoroughfare they represent, producing a shift in the perception of reality. The subsequent work is a visual analysis of a space that, though different in concept, is akin to the spatial representations that Francesca Woodman makes and which are explored by Simon in her chapter.

Like Wilkie and Pendlebury, Adam Murray and Diane Smyth provide a dialogue in their chapter *PPP: Preston, Paris, Process*. Their discussion documents a full range of issues in relation to practice, from philosophical reflections in connection to the process of the book and its potential risk and failure, to important practical matters associated with the dissemination of the book and the role that the book fair, gallery exhibition and collection play in this.

Sarah Bodman's chapter, *Imaginary Shadows: fictional documentary photography in artists' books*, considers the book as a form which carries with it an implied authenticity. Bodman presents an overview of a number of bookworks that play with this sense of authenticity and which have a particular relationship to the photograph. In part, each work that Bodman considers pays homage to another book or format (the photo album, a novel, a travelogue, or indeed other artists' books). Each book toys with what is fiction and what is fact. This is further borne out in explorations of documentary that underpin many of the discussions and examples that are considered within this book.

In the penultimate chapter, Tim Daly explores influential works in terms of notions of materiality, physicality and handling. In *Reinstating Touch in the Documentary Photobook*, Daly particularly considers the continued interest in these concerns, writing as a practitioner for whom an important motive is the continuation of the book – in part – as a sensual experience. Daly reviews a range of examples that, on one hand, link to considerations of the digital that are evident in the chapters by Kelly and Verity, but also to the past as represented in Borda's chapter.

The book ends with Lawrence George Giles' visual essay, *Memory of a Memory*. In line with Kelly's chapter which considers the development of work towards the artist's book format, Giles presents an early iteration of what will become an artist's book. The work takes as its subject matter *the book* and its material form and related ephemera – in this instance the photograph album and its contents – in order to explore the photograph and its potential to help us to remember, or, indeed, to construct memory. Giles operates within the wider context of artists who use the family album format, as Sisley explores in his chapter and as we can see in the work of Kelly and the work of Scott McCarney, featured in Bodman's chapter.

This book is presented in order to contribute to the wider discussions that encompass contemporary issues in the separate fields of photography and the artist's book. We note that these fields have been in convergence for what is now a significant period and that the products of this subsequent overlap bring to the forefront of creative visual practice a substantial heritage and a volume of work that offers a concrete area of practice which requires continued reflection, critique and analysis. The book sets out to bring these two elements and their convergence into sharper focus. Our intention here is to bring key issues to the fore that will continue to stimulate discussion and engender future study and debate; to this end we trust that the reader will enjoy the wide range of contributions that follow.

CONTEXT

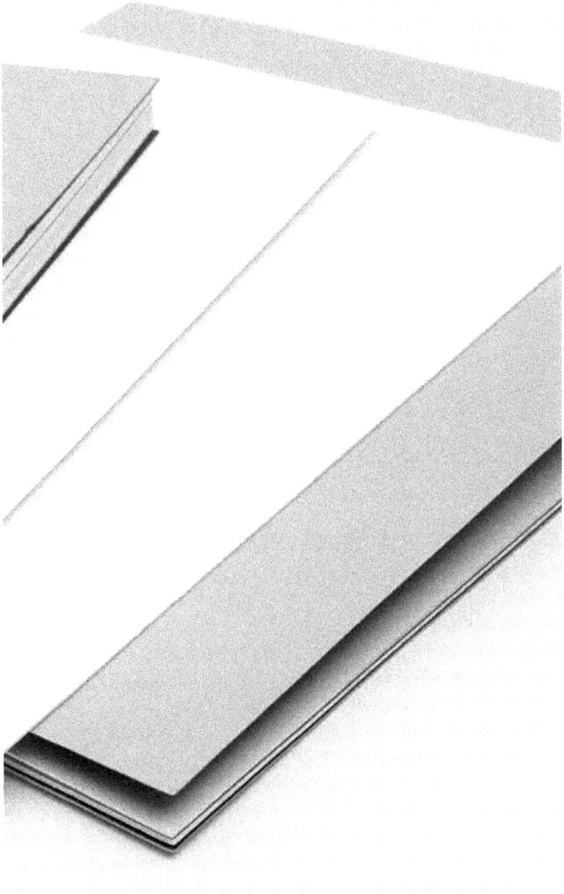

Plain Carbon Steel (detail). David Penny (2011)

The Artist's Photographic Book: Towards a Definition

SYLVIA GRACE BORDA
Emily Carr University of Art and Design
Vancouver, Canada

When considering the artist's photographic book as a genre, we cannot escape the vagueness of its classification. Defined only through its physicality and processes, the authorship behind such works is open to debate. Is, for example, a catalogue of photographs representing an artist's own opus to be included in this form? Does a book of photographs owned by an artist qualify for this title, or must the work come from the artist's own hand; if so, would a factual book illustrated photographically be eligible, or must "photography as an art form" take precedence in the publication?

In defining the artist's photographic book, I propose that it could be any of these. To illustrate this, I will provide an overview of how the development of photographic technologies and processes contributed to early print culture in the 19th century. In this context I will then examine how Anna Atkins' (1799-1871) botanical book *Photographs of British Algae: Cyanotype Impressions* (1843) resides as an author-produced photographic project; existing as an art form as well as a set of scientific reference books. By re-examining the core values and choices made by Atkins, one can start to map and understand production values associated with the artist's photographic book. Lastly I will explore how the advent of compilation-based consumer products, such as the photographic album, presented ideal conditions for the public to self-publish their own folios, and the impact this has had in defining the artist's photographic book.

Early photographic histories: a question of medium

The origin of the word *photography* is owed to Sir John Herschel (1792-1871), who coined the term in 1839. Basing the definition on how the image is recorded on paper, its etymology comes from the Greek words for light and writing. Already the premise of the artist's photographic book, as an object fitting between the visual and the literary, is not inconceivable; for photography's own nominal description alluded to the conditions and processes of writing. In turn, the concept of reading is also implied in photography's literal terms.

The history of photography is often explained primarily in the context of processes and outputs. In the work of Louis Daguerre (1787–1851) and the invention of the daguerreotype, or that of William Henry Fox Talbot (1800-1877) and his invention of the calotype, the nature of the scenes depicted is considered secondary in preference to the study of form and creation. In this way, the work of these photographers is often placed in the realm of objecthood before imagery. Indeed, since their original conception, the processes behind these photographic methods have defined the image's relationship to its publishing vehicle. A silver-coated copper plate is made sensitive to light by iodine vapours, then, transferred by a lightproof holder, the plate is placed in a camera and exposed to light. Developed by exposure to mercury vapours, the plate is fixed by a solution of sodium hyposulphite. The finished plate bears a detailed positive image through the remaining exposed and developed silver.[1] As there is no intermediary negative created throughout this process, each daguerreotype remains unique.

The potential of Daguerre's process to make exact visual records of the built and rural environment was immediately recognised and exploited by publishers – strengthening the connection of photography to the book, yet not equalling its form in terms of informational purity. The daguerreotype image could not be reproduced on the book's pages, but was instead copied through other processes such as etching, engraving or lithography. The sites, events and places to which a photographer had travelled were depicted on the page through this extra additive process. Despite being rendered through traditional methods of fine art printmaking, the daguerreotype enabled the world to be shown more objectively through early photography processes, rather than by the subjective representations of the artist's hand. Yet at the same time, this step along from the original exposure could not account for an entirely 'true' representation of the world.

The early stages of this process culminated in *Excursions daguerriennes : vues et monuments les plus remarquables de globe* [*Daguerreotype Excursions: the world's most spectacular views and monuments*], a book series published by Lerebours between 1841 and 1843 that drew on selected photographic submissions from the Mediterranean, Northern Europe, North America and Russia.[2] The publication acknowledges in its title the role of photography in informing the images; yet in reading *Excursions daguerriennes*, viewers are left to experience a book's images mediated through the labour and interpretation of lithographic plate makers that copied and re-rendered the photographic image. For all its proliferation and the relative accuracy of the copper plate's original image, the daguerreotype was not flawless in its published form.

Methodically stepping closer to the modern-day print is the calotype, a photographic process invented by Henry Fox Talbot. Dispensing with the need for highly-polished metal surfaces, this method employs paper to create both a negative and positive print. The process required the photographer to coat paper with silver iodide and a solution of silver nitrate and gallic acid.[3] After exposure, the paper was developed in a silver nitrate solution, and thereafter it became a negative for the contact printing of a positive image. Whilst the creation of a negative enabled a more direct reproduction process, the fibrous papers decreased the photo's definition. As a result, the calotype lacked the daguerreotype's crispness. Somewhat ironically, calotypes appeared closer to drawings or watercolour renderings than direct photographic representations.[4]

These pictorial qualities did, however, reflect Talbot's personal opinions on photography's key capabilities. An early supporter of photography's capacity to shift image production, distribution and management, in an 1839 presentation on the invention of photography he stated that, through photography, "every man (could be) his own printer and publisher."[5] He followed through with this principle in 1844, supporting his former valet in setting up the first photographic printing firm, where Talbot's own photographic book, *The Pencil of Nature*, was published. As the use of the calotype ran in tandem with the daguerreotype, the interlinked potential of photography and publishing became more strongly established.

With further developments in photographic technology during the 19th century, debates arose about photography's potential to alter its subject. Having been used solely as a mechanical recording device, the subjectivity of the image had not yet been reflected upon: photography was considered an artless medium, with no capacity to render itself in relationship to the human condition. The subjects depicted, the chosen photographic processes and positions on the selective truth of the image all offer insights into the aesthetic and objective values of both the photographers and society as a whole.

With the conception of the photogram, considerations of authenticity and authorship came to the forefront. Talbot first used this method successfully to print plant material. Using the calotype process, he allowed sunlight to pass though leaves placed on photosensitive paper, which when developed created a negative image. He named these images "photogenic drawings",[6] a title tellingly based more explicitly on artistry than the term "photogram" that we use today. Previously established photographic methods required the photographer and camera to negotiate an object or space. In a photogram, however, the object is the arranged entity, composed and physically manipulated on the paper. Furthermore, the absence of the camera meant a loss of its 'window' aesthetics, turning the page into a flat surface instead of a replacement eye. At the same time, however, the removal of the camera permitted a more direct contact between the subject and its medium, and the resulting image produced was on a 1:1 scale. With these things in mind, the photogram seemed to shed the more conventionally recorded data of the daguerreotype and calotype in favour of previously unexposed information.

In an attempt to explore and improve the photographic potential of metals other than silver, Herschel invented the "cyanotype" or "blueprint" in 1842.[7] Once employed in the action of the photogram, Prussian blue forms in the exposed areas through the light-based reaction of iron salts. Fixed with water, there is a simplicity to the cyanotype not afforded to a silver-based process. Like Talbot, Herschel recognised the photographic medium's potential for publishing. He demonstrated and produced a series of cyanotype images, arguing that the process could copy or re-render drawings, prints, and physical objects. Herschel's interest lay in the photo-mechanical capacities of the medium.

Through his own successes in rendering copies of etchings and other print media, he advocated it be applied more widely as a method of reproduction. As the fixed dimensions of a drawing could easily be recreated, the cyanotype process can be considered akin to a primitive photocopier. Indeed, the cyanotype represents the only first-generation photographic process that successfully moved on to address modern needs for copying. The cyanotype, better known to us as the blueprint, became the standard method for the reproduction of architectural and engineering drawings. Before this time, however, the medium played an equally significant role in enabling the production of the first photographic book series.

The 'first' unheralded artist's photographic book

Anna Atkins, a British botanist, considered photography as an alternative method of recording botanical specimens for study and image dissemination. Where previous books on the subject used hand-engraved illustrations, Atkins sought to create a record that originated directly from its subjects. This was not an isolated endeavour, as she was in fact in direct communication with Herschel and in correspondence with Talbot, who was a keen botanist himself. Atkins realised that the combined values of Talbot's photogenic print or photogram technique and Herschel's cyanotype process could offer an alternative to traditional image publishing. Rather than using letterpress and plate engravings, she could let the plants render themselves onto photographic paper.

Atkins became the first to print and self-publish a book through photography – more specifically through the cyanotype process. In 1843, she cleverly used the photogram method to transfer her handwritten text and record the silhouetted forms of her plants. Whilst realising Talbot's allusion to "every man a publisher" Atkins' own contribution to the photographic book is twofold. Concurrent to producing the first photographically-illustrated book, she also proved that individuals could print precise scientific details through photography, to form a series or set of multiple copies ready for distribution.

Atkins' publication consisted of a series of loosely-bound cyanotypes, which built up over time to form a complete handmade manuscript. As her folios were created in separate parts over the course of a decade, with their material possibly not published more than a dozen times, what makes Atkins' work similar to the artist's book is that each page had to be reset with each publication. Atkins' own invested labour, use of hand-coated cyanotype paper, and employment of the photogram process, greatly limited the reproducibility and extent of the series: each book is akin to a single edition, following the aesthetics and composition of a visual journal.

Regardless of the modest number of works printed, *British Algae: Cyanotype Impressions* was a significant publishing feat. Over a ten-year period the work was printed in small folios, which by its end amounted to over 350 cyanotype photograms.[8]

The cyanotype process required the reassembly of the book's content so each page is a singular creation. As a consequence of the need to set and re-figure content, there are variations. As such, whilst the content remains the same across each of the books' pages its composition is unique. When the books are viewed comparatively, the cyanotype process illustrates small differences between each of the specimen images. While artistry was not an intentional focus of Atkins' photographic output, it arises through her production techniques, enabling her work to be read as an artist's photographic book. Furthermore, by using her own handwriting to label each specimen plate with its Latin species and genus, Atkins' script offsets the anticipated letterpress notes one would expect to find in a commercial scientific book. Her pages become a testament to her individualistic involvement and offer a trace of herself in their production. Whilst evidence of the human hand is not necessarily required in an artistic context, it serves to separate *British Algae: Cyanotype Impressions* from similar scientific explorations.

In this manner, Atkins' work carries hints of a skilled artist-illustrator driven by both aesthetic and scientific considerations. Atkins did not elect simply to illustrate botanic structures, but to explore the aestheticism behind such a document.

Her handwritten notes were carefully crafted, and she attempted to increase the visual appeal through her imaginative specimen placement on the page. Atkins' mindful staging of specimens created dynamic positive and negative spaces. Through a compositional understanding of the process's dark ground, she attempted to foreground and frame her botanical specimens so that they flowed across the page. In this way, Atkins' use of space is as considered as the manner in which an artist might fill a page with a drawing.

And yet it is not the visual intention behind the images that gives them true artistic definition, but rather how content and composition come together. The inherent artistic nature of this book is seen where the nature of its process (including hand labour, human intervention and chemical processes) supports its material reality, whilst also aligning with its content, context and nature. The artistry of Atkins' book is also visible when one considers colour associations. Whilst the Prussian blue of the cyanotype may underline a series of forgotten Victorian visual and aesthetic sensibilities,[9] it is a colour that serendipitously aligns with its process. Having been fixed by water, the rich blue is reminiscent of the algae's original habitat; a connection visually enhanced by the image's often varying colour saturation that is a consequence of the liquid processing. Whilst water is the plant's context, it similarly determines its representation, forming a silhouette reminiscently floating in flat space. Whilst it is unlikely Victorian society would see romanticism in algae, the idea that the algae could be rendered and associated from the very depths of the waters they come from would have appealed to wider British aesthetic values at that time.

In further considering Atkins' work as an artist's photographic book, one realises the processes adopted reveal themselves in the book's title. The literary and the scientific become two tangents that are consciously named, and direct the reader's responses to this work. In *Photographs of British Algae: Cyanotype Impressions*, the titling acknowledges the imaging process, as well as the fact these pictures are a set of *impressions*, created through direct contact with the photosensitive paper. Atkins' titling is akin to devices used by conceptual photographers over a century later, in which photographers would name their work in a literal sense around activities and processes. In this way, the publication's title reveals both the activity and the process to be found within the book's pages. An example of early conceptual photography and book titling can be found in Ed Ruscha's *Twentysix Gasoline Stations* (1963). The title reveals literally what the reader will discover in the book's pages. In this work, Ruscha photographed gas stations along old Route 66 between Los Angeles and Oklahoma City. The book consists of gasoline stations with captions indicating their name and location. Comparable to the work of conceptual photographers, Atkins has also produced her botanical images without commentary. Only the name appears in print as identification of what particular species is portrayed.

These definitional tendencies are clarified in the introduction and commentary found in the first folio of the book, where Atkins establishes a context of what had been accomplished whilst also defining her intended audience:

> *The difficulty of making accurate drawings of objects as minute as many of the Algae and Confera, has induced me to avail myself of Sir John Herschel's beautiful process of Cyanotype, to obtain impressions of the plants themselves, which I have*

much pleasure in offering to my botanical friends.

I hope that in general the impressions will be found sharp and well defined, but in some instance... the thickness of the specimens it is impossible to press the glass used in the taking...

...The names refer to Harvey's "Manuel of British Algae" – I have taken the Tribes and the Species in their proper order when I was able to do so, but in many cases I have been compelled to make long gaps, from the want of the plants that should have been next inserted and in this first number I have intentionally departed from systematic arrangement that I might give... a sample.[10]

Far from the stringency of more traditional academic publications, Atkins acknowledges the methods and aesthetic value of the cyanotype process, and establishes that the book is intended for botanical friends. Her preface describes a publishing dynamic not dissimilar to the creation and promotion of artists' books, wherein copies were shared amongst subscribing colleagues and associates. This self-initiated or counter-cultural response to produce and circulate her folio to friends situates the book and the purpose of the edition. The intimacy of friendship is combined with a debatable objective science, creating a document that might sit slightly uneasily in a purely academic framework. Yet Atkins notes that she has produced her illustrated book in response to the esteemed body of work by the curator of the Trinity College Herbarium, and Professor of Botany of the Royal Dublin Society, William Henry Harvey (1811–1866). In this way Atkins' work becomes an ode to, and continuation of, Harvey's unillustrated *Manual of British Algae* (1841),[11] wherein she has now produced the illustrations to match his research. By creating an indexical series of images to complement the work of Harvey, one could argue Atkins created a conceptual strategy to legitimize her processes. What is meant here by conceptual strategy is that Atkins prepared a self-initiated brief and specifically undertook an independent project to illustrate Harvey's manual. Throughout the work, Atkins asserted her botanical knowledge and skills that resulted in not only complementing Harvey's published research but at the same time extending scientific and botanical knowledge of the era.

Perhaps by virtue of the images' isolation

from their documented text, in Atkins' work the subjectivity of the cyanotype becomes all the more apparent through its condensed form. Yet alongside this, *Photographs of British Algae: Cyanotype Impressions* simultaneously exposed the medium's objective qualities. The scaled picture of the photogram process suited scientific illustration better than hand-rendered drawings, not just in terms of physical accuracy to the original form, but in its working process. The photogram is authored not through direct human interpretation but by science itself, through nature and light.

It should be noted that in Atkins' *Photographs of British Algae*, the final binding and collation of the plates was left to the subscriber. In the 19th century it was anticipated that loosely-bound materials would be sent for bookbinding at the subscriber's own cost. Consequently, the subscriber could control its exterior aesthetic, binding their materials in leathers to complement their own private library. This method also permitted the subscriber control over the arrangement of Atkins' material. Whilst the ability to remove, study closely or rearrange Atkins' folios could enhance the recipient's scientific study, at the same time it produced a more interactive informational format between the author and reader. Atkins would issue replacement plates for specimens published, sometimes resulting in significant variation between her book copies: certain editions could contain more than 400 plates rather than 389. Again, similar to an artist, Atkins had a particular relationship with her photographic books, considering them open to editing and revising. Indeed, self-publishing permitted a freedom of content not seen in other distribution methods, and as such was a practice adopted by many 19th century authors. If writers could pay for the costs of typesetting their own book titles, they would be sent to press. Authors such as William Blake (1757-1827) and Lewis Carroll (1832-1898) adopted 'vanity' publishing to produce a limited edition book for close friends, and as a method through which to manage their own book distribution and to take control of profit.

The development of photographic books and prints

Through the 19th century, the concept of photography as an artistic medium would remain in question. In the rapid popularisation and industrialisation of the daguerreotype, followed by the calotype, collodion and other subsequent photographic processes, critics and artists alike were forced to create and support a definition of art that either categorically excluded the new photographic medium or wholeheartedly included it.[12] As most art forms of the time were valued for their lengthy processes and visible craftsmanship, photography's foothold in 'real life' and its rapidity of process guaranteed that there were many opponents to seeing the medium as an art form.

Since photography required limited human intervention to record an image, the medium was initially defined as a mechanical process. What proponents of photography as a mechanical means exalted were its so-called 'truthful' accuracies. The thoughts of American author, amateur photographer and innovator Oliver Wendell Holmes (1809-1894) on the difference between a photograph – not photographer – and an artist are as follows:

> *The very things which an artist would leave out, or render imperfectly, the photograph takes infinite care with, and so makes its illusions perfect...*
>
> *This is one infinite charm of the photographic delineation. Theoretically, a perfect photograph is*

> *absolutely inexhaustible. In a picture you can find nothing which the artist has not seen before you; but in a perfect photograph there will be as many beauties lurking, unobserved, as there are flowers that blush unseen in forests and meadows. It is a mistake to suppose one knows a... picture when he has studied it a hundred times by the aid of the best of our common instruments. Do we know all that there is in a landscape by looking out at it from our parlour-windows?* [13]

Whilst technological and industrial advancements during the 19th century were considered overwhelming, their capacities to add to art production were merely regarded as an observational complement. In this manner, even today, Atkins' adoption of photographic processes and incorporation of botanical subject matter in her books firmly and inadvertently places them within the categories of science exploration and learning rather than art. What Atkins' books explicitly offered the reader was a set of collated photographic reference materials. Whilst this format was time-consuming to produce through hand-coating papers, printing of specimen images and binding, other photographic processes were emerging. The rapid commercialization of photographic processes created a public eager to consume images of both themselves and far-off places.

It should be noted that photographic studios grew quickly during the years of Atkins' photographic book production (1842-1852). These studios often did not produce paper-based images like Atkins but first subscribed to the daguerreotype process. The very nature of the daguerreotype as an irreproducible, singular image was limiting and disadvantageous for clients and photographers alike. Though calotype printing could enable duplication, it was equally considered a poor choice, since materials seemed to lack the mirror-like definition found in the daguerreotype process.

With escalating client demand, the photographic industries sought ways to improve photographic processes and outputs. By 1848 Fredrick Scott Archer (1813-1857) had invented an alternative photographic process, whereby a photographic emulsion suspended in an ionized wet collodion solution is applied onto glass. Through the "wet collodion" process the glass substrate did not interfere with the image recording process, and was advantageous in having a fast emulsion for recording the chosen subject. Also, unlike the earlier calotype process, there was no interference from recording and printing out the paper's fibres. As such, the wet collodion process offered imaging comparable to early daguerreotype processes, but now with a capacity for the image to be easily replicated and duplicated on demand.[14]

By the early 1850s, the wet collodion process was overwhelmingly adopted, nearly resulting in the demise of the daguerreotype by the decade's end. With such an increase in the output and popularity of collodion prints, there was an instant marketplace for the sale and merchandising of images as keepsakes and collectibles. Professional photographers began to create a mounted stock of photographic prints, illustrating everything from the reigning monarch to landscapes. These images were initially sold by booksellers and stationers, alongside chemists that sold raw photographic chemicals, and railway station kiosks associated with domestic tourist destinations. With this came the introduction of the photographic album, which enabled the wider public to become editors of their own photo book. Collecting photographic images and assembling albums became part of a new visual cultural phenomenon, revolutionized by a more accessible and affordable photographic medium. With photographic images displayed for sale in windows and on racks outside shops, the printed image proliferated and became increasingly commoditised.

The public's ability to self-select, purchase, and curate commercially-bought images can be paralleled both by artists and "vanity" authors. The process mirrors a published artist's selection of found content, while the investment and purchasing power of an album-maker illustrates values similar to those of vanity authors. Indeed, there was a great willingness on the part of the public to spend their money forming collections that could be used as illustrative platforms, demonstrating a desire to involve themselves in representations. In particular albums often displayed travel tours that their authors had undertaken. Whilst the photography apparatus was inaccessible for many tourists to buy, let alone operate, bought images could act as both a memento of their journey and a physical sign of the traveller's cultural and financial affluence. The album format grew out of already existing bookmaking practices. Photographic albums were like sketchbooks, sold as bound journals that offered their reader/owner a set number of pages and slots to insert mounted images. Album owners added their own information such as dates, locations, or travel routes across the pages or photographs themselves, in a manner not dissimilar to Atkins' printing out her own handwritten notes across her specimen book pages. Personification of the album became an extension of self-authoring and assertion of accomplishments – whether observational notes, or simply a compilation of lists of people and places visited.

The capacity of photography to record tourist sites is well described by Oliver Wendell Holmes in June 1859. Holmes' article addresses photography's proliferation, but equally alludes to the fact that photographic representation can situate the viewer beyond their immediate place and experience. Holmes wrote:

> *Form is henceforth divorced from matter. In fact, matter as a visible object is of no great use any longer, except as the mould on which form is shaped. Give us a few negatives of a thing worth seeing,*

> *taken from different points of view, and that is all we want of it...*
>
> *...There is only one Coliseum or Pantheon; but how many millions of potential negatives have they shed, – representatives of billions of pictures, – since they were erected! Matter in large masses must always be fixed and dear; form is cheap and transportable. We have got the fruit of creation now, and need not trouble ourselves with the core. Every conceivable object of Nature and Art will soon scale off its surface for us. Men will hunt all curious, beautiful, grand objects, as they hunt the cattle in South America, for their skins, and leave the carcasses as of little worth.*[15]

Bound blank books created for personalisation purposes were already in existence before the 19th century's proliferation of the photo album. From the 15th century, commonplace books emerged as a way to compile information including but not limited to recipes, quotations, letters and poems. They graphically and textually illustrated a creator's particular interests, evolving over the centuries to include friendship albums, and book editions that permitted grangerisation – a format wherein published stories had blank pages included at the end, allowing their owners to add their own notes.[16]

Thus the concept of scrapbooking was already part of 19th century media and print culture. The scrapbook album itself could be bought permanently bound, or loose-leaf with the ability to allow for insertion of pages. Scrapbooks also arose as a medium marketed in tandem with photo albums, to encourage the public to collect, curate and create their own personalised photographic books. In this way, early photographic scrapbooks and albums were precursors of the artist's photographic book, offering the reader a new position from which to manage content presented in a book format. Similarly, they were considered self-authored works, and carried appropriate social gravitas. Such books were often monogrammed and personalised across the covers and binding, further strengthening the relationship of the work to author and owner. In the 21st century, scrapbooks and albums continue to provide users a format from which to build personal and visual narratives. The notion of the album has also continued to evolve and shift through new media forms but personification remains a critical element. The rise of the blog is a notable example of images and text coexisting in a context of personal relevance, naming (e.g. through URL naming) and expression.

The artist's photographic book and the photographically illustrated book

In this context the botanical illustration, as seen in Atkins' work, entered a no-man's-land in that there was no precedence in its form. What was it? What was its purpose? When considering botanical illustration, whether drawn or produced through photography, its definition lies between art and science. It seems to allude to the paradox of an artist's photographic book offering many different platforms for use, readership and dissemination. Similarly the artist's photographic book classification remains complicated, simultaneously defined as illustrative literature, catalogue, scientific aid, and/or an independent unit of experience. Hence, the photographic or artist-determined book remains in flux, and can be placed across many categories, and equally considered as not readily defined by any. Expanding upon photography's early illustration of nature and scientific principles, the photographically illustrated and artist's photographic book play a significant role in expanding knowledge and stimulating wider cultural debates. The book has always had an advantage in that, unlike an exhibition, it was portable and reproducible: several book copies could be available and read by the public across various geographies and time zones.

In the absence of any one categorisation available through visual art or scientific terms, what one finds is that the power of the artist's photographic books arises as a medium which can bridge so many experiences and definitions.

While it may be an oversimplification in describing how photographic works are authored, there appears to be a set of three common conditions. In the first condition, the artist-author must collate and consider how content will be presented, and in what context. In this manner, the book format asserts a particular aesthetic position of the artist-author. In its second state, the book as concept becomes a production and editorial process; it will require assembly, art, and editorial direction. Thirdly, the book becomes an output; that is, the book becomes an independent unit of information, gaining meaning and agency through its use and changing values across time.

One could debate whether Anna Atkins' botanical books, or the independently authored photographic albums from the 1850s-1890s, are solely representative of a certain type of small press authorship. There is still the question of where these publications belong as a genre. What can be drawn from the successes of these early folios and one-off albums, in combination with the common conditions of authorship outlined above, is that they can provide the contemporary artist-maker with a rudimentary set of defining guidelines. These guidelines can support how artists' photographic books might be defined and recognised within the contemporary marketplace as a distinct genre and expression of artistic endeavour. Guidelines might, for instance, encompass a defined use and adoption by the artist/author of a means of photographic reproduction; a research-led or innovative approach that results in a composition in book form that has photographically illustrated components supporting contextual information related to one or more themes; and the use of text to complement, add tension to, or create new meaning between what is photographically represented and what is stated. As an overarching guideline, the artist's photographic book or photographically illustrated book provides a platform for the artist's/author's illustration of his or her own photographic studies, artistic interests or personal expressions. They offer a renewed sensitivity to the artist's/author's perceptions, and particularly to a sense of place; and not least to the idea of how image(s) can be used as active agents for representation in lieu of language or words. In addition to such defining guidelines is a concerted fostering of awareness in the marketplace and within scholarship of the positioning of the artist's photographic book within a value scheme.

Thus far, what defines an artist's photographic book is exactly what defies it. The artist's photographic book is illustrated by photographs, and likewise may or may not be produced by a photographer. Like Anna Atkins' photographic books, the placement of the images and their composition give resonance and context to the content of the work. It should be noted that, like Atkins, successful photographically illustrated books, particularly when first appearing in public view, might not have been aligned with artistic intent. The varied approaches to the production and form of the artist's photographic book itself brings into reflection our own sensibilities – what we value, accept, and reject as important to be read, exhibited and preserved. Perhaps inevitably, time and new technological processes will continue to act as agencies which shift how the artist's photographic book will be shaped as a medium. Likewise, time, cultural and material aesthetics will equally alter how the artist's photographic book continues to be defined and contested as a work of art or literature.[17]

NOTES

1 Definition in: http://www.moma.org/modernteachers/glossary.html Accessed 4 Mar. 2012.

2 Eleanor Brown, "The world's first daguerreotype images – Canadian travel photographer Pierre Gustave Gaspard Joly de Lotbinière", *The Archivist: Magazine of the National Archives of Canada*, No. 118, 1999.

3 Harry John Philip Arnold, *William Henry Fox Talbot pioneer of photography and man of science* (London: Hutchinson Benham, 1977), 18.

4 Alan Greene, *Primitive Photography: A Guide to Making Cameras, Lenses, and Calotypes* (Boston: Focal Press, 2002), 4.

5 Geoffrey Batchen *William Henry Fox Talbot* (London: Phaidon Press, 2008).

6 Roger Taylor, *Impressed by Light: British Photographs from Paper Negatives*, 1840-1860 (New York: Metropolitan Museum of Art Press, 2007).

7 Mike Ware, *Cyanotype: the history, science and art of photographic printing in Prussian blue*. (London: Science Museum UK, 1999).

8 Alexandra Botelho, *A Survey of Early Photographically Illustrated Books: 1839-1852, Including an Account of the Volumes Present in the George Eastman House Library Rare Book Collection*, (New York: George Eastman House – Photograph Conservation, 2002).

9 Sylvia Borda, "Pictorialist Vocabularies – Colour Meaning and Processes,' In *H.G. Cox: British Columbia pictorialist* (North Vancouver: Presentation House Gallery Press, 2004).

10 "Ocean Flowers: Anna Atkins's Cyanotypes of British Algae."
Page transcription by author of Anna Atkin's book preface found at New York Public Library 20 Mar. 2012
http://digitalgallery.nypl.org/nypldigital/id?419691.

11 Clíodhna Ní Bhroin, Botanist at the Royal Botanic Gardens, Edinburgh, Personal interview about Botanical science and its context to Anna Atkins' processes in *Photographs of British Algae: Cyanotype Impressions*, 31 Mar. 2012.

12 "About Charles Baudelaire, On Photography, from The Salon of 1859" Accessed 2 Apr. 2012
http://www.csus.edu/indiv/o/obriene/art109/readings/11%20baudelaire%20photography.htm

13 *The Atlantic*, Volume 3. Accessed 28 Mar. 2012.
http://www.theatlantic.com/magazine/archive/1859/06/the-stereoscope-and-the-stereograph/3361/

14 Martha Langford "A Short History of the Photographic Album 1860–1960" Accessed 10 Mar. 2012
http://www.mccord-museum.qc.ca/en/keys/virtualexhibits/notmanstudio/themes/albums/

15 *The Atlantic*, Volume 3. Accessed 28 Mar. 2012
http://www.theatlantic.com/magazine/archive/1859/06/the-stereoscope-and-the-stereograph/3361/

16 Johanna Drucker, *The Century of Artists' Books* (New York: Granary Books, 1995).

17 The author extends gratitude to Dorothy A Hunter for her editorial guidance.

Locating Photography and the Artist's Book

THERESA WILKIE
School of Art & Design
University of Salford

JANE PENDLEBURY
Special Collections
Manchester Metropolitan University

To situate the reader of this volume not only in the production of the photographic artist's book, but also in the manner in which we might consume it, this chapter this chapter will explore the Artists' Book Collection at Manchester Metropolitan University Special Collections (MMU Special Collections) – in particular the artists' books which consciously use photography. Artists' books form more than a tenth of the Book Design Collection at MMU Special Collections and although the books are housed separately to the main library they are open to the public and can be browsed.

We explore the Artists' Book Collection by offering two voices; that of the collector and the user. Jane Pendlebury, Senior Library Assistant in Special Collections, will discuss the beginning of the collection, its range, and how it is used. She will also discuss the collecting policy and how it has reflected the changing nature of the artist's book over the last 50 years. Theresa Wilkie will discuss her experience of using the collection, both as a student and more recently with Plot, a group of artists and writers interested in using photography and the book to explore public interaction with landscape, environment and place. Our intention here is to explore the development of artists' books using photography within the collection and also to record a dialogue about what constitutes an artist's book or a photobook and how the two come together.

The collector

The artists' books at MMU Special Collections number over 2,000 items and range in scope from the 1960s to the present day. The collection has great breadth and all categories of artists' books are actively collected. The emphasis is on British artists, though American and other international artists are also represented. The collection originated in the early 1970s when artists' multiples were acquired by Gaye Smith, the art librarian at the time. They were acquired as part of the normal stock selection and she has noted how they were "treated like the rest of the lending stock and were dog-eared and battered as a result".[1]

It is indicative of changing attitudes towards the genre that as artists' books came to be recognised as valuable art objects the need to conserve them for future use became paramount. At MMU Special Collections, the artists' books were gathered together and transferred from the general library stock to form a separate sequence within the Book Design collection. This collection of approximately 13,000 books embraces the book as an artefact, with books being purchased for their design in addition to their content. It forms part of MMU Special Collections, which in 2005 were designated accredited museum status by the Museum Libraries and Archives Council.

The fact that the artists' books now form part of a special collection, housed in a temperature-controlled room and for reference use only, ensures their safe keeping but could also be looked upon as a subversion of the democratising imperative which drove the emergence of the genre. This is a view acknowledged by Gaye Smith who saw the removal of books from the lending stock which were "intended for popular distribution by their creators" as "ironical".[2]

Despite this, artists' books within a library setting remain an area where library staff can facilitate access to this particular art-form and, at MMU, the books – though forming part of the special collections – remain on open shelves and are still fully browsable. The books are also in the online catalogue and are available for all to use, thus remaining true to the democratic impulse that lies behind much of artists' publishing. The staff encourage use of the books through exhibitions and teaching sessions and as a result the collection is heavily used. (The majority of people using it are art and design students, either on an individual basis or as part of a group, from Manchester Metropolitan University and other universities and colleges in the North-West of England.)

The copy of Ed Ruscha's *Twentysix Gasoline Stations* from 1962 (Figure 1) provides a perfect example of the "dog-eared" treatment that Gaye Smith refers to. This book, as the name suggests, contains 26 images of gasoline stations on the highways between Los Angeles and Oklahoma City, a journey frequently made by Ruscha. This was Ruscha's first book and is a seminal part of the collection. The cover of the book bears the scars of spine labels and the title page is littered with library stamps. Such treatment seems shocking now but could also be viewed as a testament to the levels of availability and distribution which Ruscha aspired to. Allowing the books to circulate freely enabled art, in book form, to be widely disseminated. As Stephen Bury points out:

> *The first printing was an edition of 400 numbered*

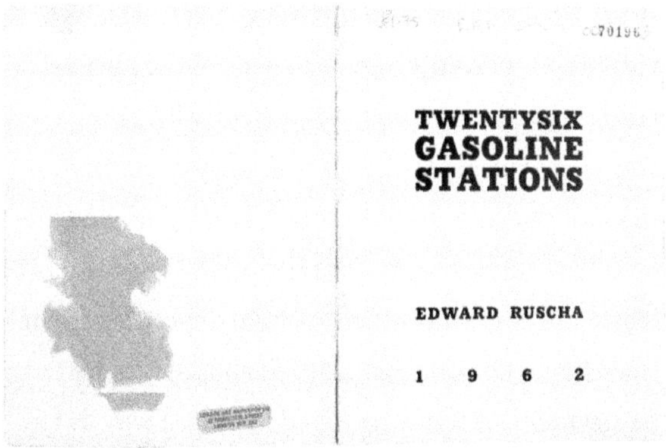

Figure 1: Ed Ruscha, (1962) Twentysix Gasoline Stations. *Alhambra: Cunningham Press. © Ed Ruscha.*

> *copies – the only one (at least so far) published by Ruscha in the tradition of the limited edition. The second was of 500 copies and the third, 3,000 as Ruscha aspired to the availability of the book in the garage store perhaps attached to one of those photographed.*[3]

Sometimes students ask to view the work of a particular artist, but in the main they search the collection thematically. Although they will draw upon all types of artists' books, in some instances photobooks are particularly relevant. For example, the photobooks produced by land artists such as Richard Long and Hamish Fulton are popular with students looking for inspiring ways in which to view and record their experiences of the natural landscape. Long's book, *A Day's Walk Past the Standing Stones of Penwith Peninsula* was published in 1980. This diminutive concertina book, just a couple of inches high, contains nine black and white photographs of large Cornish boulders. The *leperello*, or concertina, form enables the book to be stood on end and arranged in such a way as to create a miniature but nevertheless impressive "stone circle". It is an interesting example for students because it demonstrates how the structure of the book, in this case the concertina, can be used to great effect in combination with the content to convey meaning. In several other works Long exploits another aspect of the book form – its sequential nature – in order to document journeys.

The photobook is the perfect vehicle for recording the temporal nature of a walk or for capturing art made along the way, and Hamish Fulton is another artist who exploits this to great effect. *Bird Song*, published in 1991, is a catalogue designed by Hamish Fulton to accompany an exhibition at the Serpentine Gallery. Within it, Fulton integrates text and image in a series of black-and-white and colour photographs with superimposed typography. For example, in one image the details of seventeen walks within a circular walk are laid over a close-up colour image of foliage and crops. The book not only chronicles walks which Fulton has made but turns them into works of art with which we can engage.

A number of teaching sessions are offered by MMU Special Collections staff aimed at introducing students to the medium of the artist's book. In these instances, staff will usually provide students with a cross sample of books including items from the significant subset of the photobook. The selection might include influential works by Ruscha, or other books that stand as early examples within the development of the genre. Telfer Stokes is an artist who has been using the artist's book as a primary medium since the early 1970s and MMU Special Collections has several of his bookworks in the collection. Stokes describes his publications in terms of the "exploration of the book form to structure visual narrative" [4] and he achieves this through the relationship of images and the sequencing of pages. *Passage* is a small photographic book published in an edition of 1,000 in 1972. (Figure 2) In this example, the effect of the sandwich being

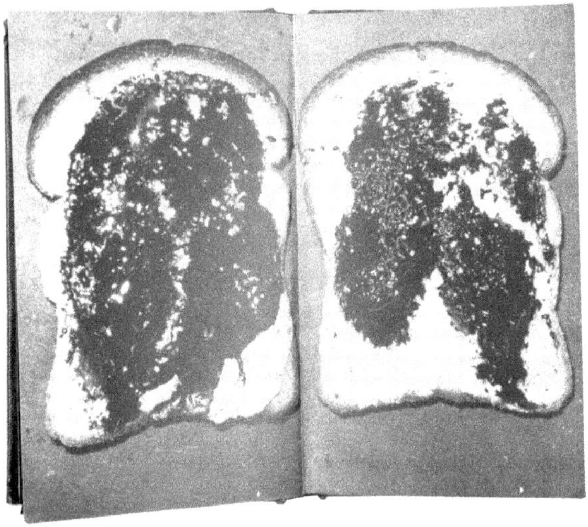

Figure 2: Telfer Stokes (1972) Passage. *UK: Weproductions © Telfer Stokes, Weproductions.*

torn apart and put together could not be attained, outside of the original object and with the integrity achieved, in anything other than a book.

Sequence is used inventively by other book artists exploring the potential of the book as a complete art object. *Illiers Combray*, published by Helen Douglas and Zoe Irvine in 2004, is another book published under the Weproductions imprint established by Telfer Stokes in 1971 and joined by Douglas in 1974 (Figure 3). Douglas and Irvine, inspired by a visit to the town immortalised by Proust, produced a two-sided concertina of

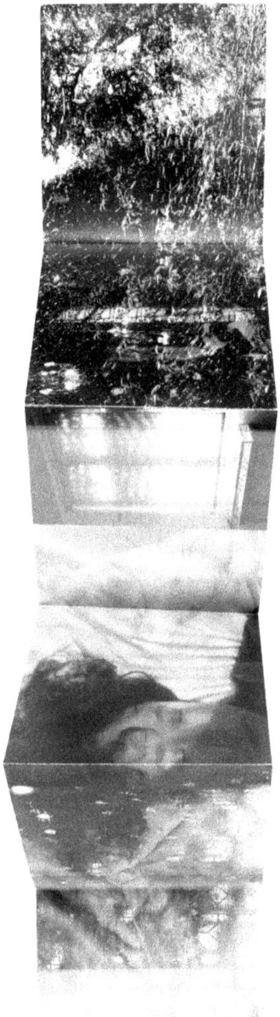

Figure 3: Helen Douglas and Zoe Irvine (2004) Illiers Combray. *Scotland: Weproductions © Helen Douglas, Weproductions.*

120 pages which contains overlapping highly coloured images which in their own words create an "ornately interwoven visual narrative... exploring a sense of memory and place".[5]

Such material is of interest not only to students investigating the creative potential of sequence within books, but also to those interested in the themes of location and memory, both popular topics amongst our students. The fact that artists' books can be approached from so many different angles is indicative of their multi-faceted nature and their value as an inspirational resource within a library setting. The students using the collection come from across all areas of art and design and we might show books produced by artists who are primarily sculptors, painters, installation artists, conceptual artists or fine art photographers. Such books demonstrate to students working in different areas of art practice how the book form can be deployed to great effect.

Sol LeWitt's book *Autobiography*, published in 1980, is another influential book within the collection and the genre. It has a grid format with nine photographs per page. In total there are around a thousand images which catalogue LeWitt's personal possessions, thus providing a visual inventory of the artist's living and working space. This book is often used as an example in teaching sessions as it demonstrates how the photographic book can provide an inventive and highly effective alternative to the written book. Sol LeWitt's *Autobiography* is not autobiographical in a traditional literary sense: there are no written words, but from the objects that surround him we gain a sense of his life. Of interest here is the section of the book where he catalogues his own book collection. On one page there are two images of Richard Long's book *A Days Walk Past the Standing Stones of Penwith Peninsula* (referred to previously), one of the front cover and the other of the book opened out. Long's book had been published just two years before *Autobiography*.

Sometimes artists use the book as a means of 'capturing' their work. Galleries provide a temporary space for artworks to be exhibited while, in contrast, an accompanying book offers the artist a more permanent medium with a higher level of distribution. *Kaddish* by Christian Boltanski accompanied his exhibition held at the Musée d'Art Moderne in Paris in 1998. It is, however, more than an exhibition catalogue. The Kaddish is the Hebrew prayer for the dead and the book itself resembles a gravestone: it is heavy, stone coloured, the pages are dark. There is no text, only a collection of found photographs which include portraits of families at leisure alongside images of German soldiers from the second world war and images of displaced, orphaned children and deceased people. One double spread contrasts a blurred close up of a child with an image of two small boys laughing and playing in a domestic interior. By juxtaposing these images, Boltanski forces the reader to recall and confront the darker periods of our shared history and, in the blurring of many of the images, he illustrates the fading of memories and perhaps also challenges our collective desire to forget. Presenting the work in book form permits these juxtapositions, and parallels our personal experiences of the photographic album (a form familiar to us all).

Such books might be considered mass produced, rather than original artworks, thus opening up the debate of what does, or does not, constitute an artist's book. In a catalogue accompanying an exhibition of artists' books held at MMU in 1993, Gaye Smith drew attention to this ambiguity and spoke of how a "liberal interpretation of *artist's book*" had been adopted

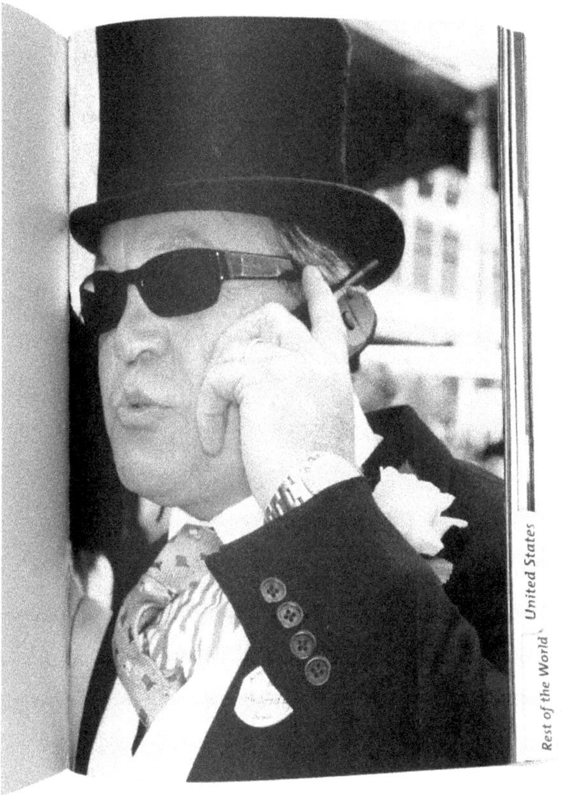

Figure 4: Martin Parr (2002). Phone Book. *London: Rocket. Martin Parr/Magnum Photos.*

during the selection process for the exhibition in order to include "those artists to whom the book is an important medium of expression".[6]

Our collecting policy likewise is built upon a similarly broad interpretation, thus enabling us to acquire books and build a collection that encompasses the diverse nature of the genre. It is also part of our collecting policy to ensure that current and former staff and students are represented. *Phone Book* by Martin Parr was published in 2002 in an edition of 2,002 (Figure 4). Parr has designed the book to resemble a real phone directory – it has the same cover design and is printed on newsprint but in content it differs entirely: there are no phone numbers but instead a collection of 141 colour documentary photographs of individuals from around the world using their mobile phones. Parr offers the reader a set of images which allow an observation of culture through the global use of the mobile phone. As well as being an alumnus of MMU, Martin Parr is also widely known, and showing materials to students which has been produced by artists whose names they recognise can be a useful starting point and route in for them to use the collection further.

In teaching sessions staff will also, where possible, show examples of the most recent acquisitions. The collection policy is to acquire books that will be of interest and use and which also mark new directions within the genre or augment existing strands within the collection.

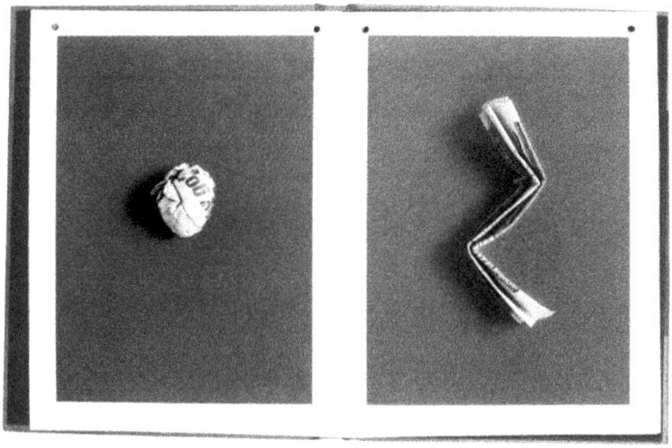

Figure 5: Stephen Gill (2008). A Series of Disappointments. *London: Nobody books. © Stephen Gill.*

Photographic works are no exception. Several books by Stephen Gill, a photographer who publishes through his own imprint, Nobody books, have recently been purchased. Gill's books are widely acknowledged as important contributions to contemporary artists' books using photography. For him, the physicality of the book – its cover, paper, texture – is as important as the content, and he established Nobody books in order to oversee every stage of the development and distribution of his publications. The books he publishes can be seen as a continuation of his photographic practice which, as Melissa Miles points out, can in turn be seen as part of a wider trend known as Conceptual Documentary which concerns itself with repetition and seriality.[7]

A Series of Disappointments, published in 2008, is a large concertina and the book block can be removed from the cover (Figure 5). It comprises a collection of photographs of discarded betting slips from betting shops in Hackney, each image generating a narrative of its own and carrying an emotional charge – one can sense the tension and disappointment in each piece of discarded paper – a screwed up ball or a more considered zigzag. The way in which the book is constructed enables the pages to be removed and hung on a wall in the manner of an exhibition.

At these teaching sessions, students are not only given an introduction to artists' books but to material that feeds into themes and topics which they will often return to investigate throughout the course of their studies. They are introduced to a source of inspiration for their own work. Sometimes, of course, photography itself is the theme and any survey of the photobooks within the collection will reveal not only interesting examples of photographic technique or innovation, but will also expose for investigation the relationship between photography and the artist's book. Indeed, it is possible, given the time in which our collection originated (not long after Ed Ruscha's early influential works) to trace the progress of this relationship through the development of the collection. Books have been acquired since the very early days of book art and the fluidity of our collecting policy has meant that we have responded not only to student needs but to developments and changes within the genre.

The user

In 2010, whilst working on a collaborative artist's book project, I visited MMU Special Collections a number of times to research and draw influence from the Book Design and Artists' Book collection. It was wonderful to be able to browse and handle such a wide range of books, those from well-known artists such as Ed Ruscha and Sophie Calle, as well as works previously unknown to me. With my collaborators, I made use of the collection in two distinct but related ways. Firstly, to research books which made a significant use of the photograph and, secondly, to examine ways in which artist's books or bookworks were constructed. In producing this book, questions were asked about why had we conceived of our project firstly as a book rather than an exhibition and also what did it mean to be doing this kind of work and why? In our project we wanted to encourage the viewer to assume an active, perhaps investigative, role and the book seemed an excellent solution for us – a format that invited the kind of investigation we sought.

I have had an interest in the photographic book and the photo essay going back to the first time, as a student, I saw Bill Brandt's *The English at Home* (1936) in this collection along with Stefan Lorant's magazine, *Lilliput* (1937-1960) – both of which use the technique of juxtaposition to create further meaning to that which we might understand if we viewed the image without its partner. Whilst *Lilliput* wasn't a photography book *per se*, it had a regular feature of a photographic juxtaposition which became known as *doubles*, usually with a humorous intention. For instance, a muscle-bound Australian serviceman next to a kangaroo, both standing upright with their arms in the same position and both subtitled *Australian*; or Neville Chamberlain juxtaposed with a llama both baring their teeth and subtitled, respectively, *Chamberlain* and *The Beautiful Llama*.

The English at Home, however, was concerned with exploring social class in British society. It

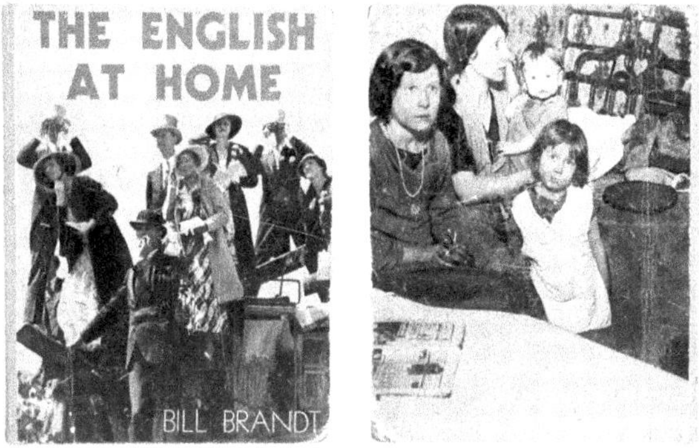

Figure 6: Bill Brandt (1936). The English at Home. *London: Batsford. © Bill Brandt Archive.*

was Brandt's first book and was published in 1936 by Batsford. It was sold for five shillings and, according to a letter written by Brandt to his publisher, it eventually had to be remaindered.[8] It was published as a hardback book, 235mm in height and 190mm in width, and contained a series of 63 photographs which attempted to highlight class in England. Juxtaposing images brought out stark social contrasts. The front and back covers juxtapose a wealthy, well-dressed group at leisure, enjoying the races, with a working class family group in an unkempt domestic interior – the mother averting her eyes from the camera (Figure 6). Inside the book, the same rather cramped family interior is contrasted with a miner working underground.

A particularly powerful juxtaposition is that of *Dinner is Served*, (published elsewhere under the title *Parlourmaid and Under-Parlourmaid*) positioned opposite an exterior image entitled *Regency Homes in Mayfair.* Whilst this at first seems just a gentle prod at the conventions of the English upper classes, as David Campany has recently pointed out, the head parlourmaid's facial expression could actually be read as hostile or resentful. A reading of the image by photographer Nigel Henderson, cited by both Mark Haworth-Booth, in an introduction to a later book by Brandt (1977), and by Campany, in an essay about this image (2006), is worth quoting again here:

> *In [Brandt's] marvellous photograph the two house parlourmaids, prepared to wait at table, have eyes loaded like blunderbusses. Their starched caps and cuffs, their poker backs, mirror the terrible rectitude of learned attitudes. They have the same irritated loathing in defence of caste that shows in portraits of Evelyn Waugh.*[9]

In addition, Richard Howells has argued that both the parlourmaid and under-parlourmaid are "solidly proud – and even defensive – of their positions".[10] The juxtaposition in the book continues with contrasts such as the working class street and the middle class interior as depicted in the images *East End Playground in a Terraced Street* and *Kensington Children's Party*.

Looking at *The English at Home* again in this collection has engaged me in a further consideration about the nature of artists' books, and also the cataloguing of books in MMU Special Collections. For example, *The English at Home* is catalogued in Book Design, not in the Artist's Book section. Perhaps this is evidence of changing perspectives on what constitutes an 'artist's book' or 'photo book' or 'book work' (as referred to above by Gaye Smith in the context of them being treated as lending stock). In Martin Parr and Gerry Badger's book, *The Photobook: A History volume 1* (2004), they offer Ralph Prins' definition as a possibility:

> *A photobook is an autonomous art form, comparable with a piece of sculpture, a play or a film. The photographs lose their own photographic character as things 'in themselves' and become parts, translated into printing ink, of a dramatic event called a book.* [11]

Parr and Badger then go on to discuss the way in which they themselves have defined and selected photobooks for inclusion in their book (it is interesting to note they include *The English at Home* in this volume). Their definition focuses on a "specific theme" [12] or "intent" [13] but they qualify this definition as potentially being "as broad as the universe [...] or as narrow as close-ups of rippled mud".[14] Parr and Badger emphasise that the photobook is a "ragged and sprawling subject"[15] much akin to Gaye Smith's "liberal interpretation" of collecting at MMU.

Alexander Streitberger has recently pointed out that artist's books can often be seen as "in-between" different artistic genres and for me this is why they are so appealing and often definition defying. In the introduction to a special issue of the journal *Image & Narrative, Photography and the book*, and in relation to the use of photography in artists' books he states:

> *Common strategies in artist's books are, for instance, to base fictional narratives on documentary photographs taken out of their contexts, to use photographs in artists books in order to document an event, to trace an activity*

> *or to visualise an artistic concept and to compose typological series of the everyday. All these examples have in common an equivoque, ambivalent use of photographs. On a structural level, the interstices between the images and the act of turning the page are often used to leave in suspense the photographic image between reproduction of the real and the imaginary fiction.*[16]

For many, the draw of the artist's book or photobook is to rescue or situate their work outside of the constraints of the gallery and to make their work more mobile and portable, more intimate, or to have more control. This, in turn, will be affected by whether the work is singular or a multiple. Ed Ruscha, for instance, described his books as "hot art":[17]

> *I liked the idea that my books would disorient, and it seemed to happen that people would look at them and the books would seem very familiar, yet they were like a wolf in sheep's clothing.*[18]

The idea of the "wolf in sheep's clothing" could perhaps also refer back to *The English at Home*, its seemingly gentle juxtapositioning leaving a bitter taste of inequality.

Artist's books using photography, as the writers and artists referred to above point out, can be slippery and do not lend themselves to any easy definition. Indeed, perhaps it is not useful to look for one, rather the genre should be encouraged to breathe and expand. In this respect, the artists' book collection at MMU Special Collections is representative and dynamic. It forms a rich and versatile resource able to meet the needs of a wide range of users whilst supporting research into the various debates and issues that surround the genre of the artist's book, and within it the use of the photograph in book form. This is a significant location where practice, production, discovery and interaction converge; an intersection of great importance for all who are engaged in this format.

NOTES

1 Smith, G (2007) 'Artists' Books: A New Canon', in McDowall & Taylor (2007) *Special Collections*, Leeds: Wild Pansy Press p.27.

2 Ibid.

3 Bury, S (2009) *The Photo-book as Artist's Book*, Conference Paper, Arlis/Norden Conference, Moderna Museet, Stockholm, June 2009, accessed online 25/8/2011 at: www.reframing photography.com/resources/photobooks

4 Stokes, T (nd) Weproductions, accessed online at: http://Weproductions.com on 15/10/2012.

5 Douglas, H & Irvine, Z (nd) Weproductions, accessed online at: http://Weproductions.com on 15/10/2012.

6 Smith, G (1993) *Artists' Books: catalogue of the collection in The Manchester Metropolitan University Library*, Manchester: The Manchester Metropolitan University Library.

7 Miles, M (2010) 'The Drive to Archive: Conceptual Documentary Photobook Design', *Photographies*, 3:1,49-69, accessed online at: http://dx.doi.org/10.1080/17540760903561108 on 26/2/2011.

8 Campany, D (2006) The career of a photographer, the career of a photograph: Bill Brandt's art of the document, in *Making History: Art and Documentary in Britain from 1929 to Now*, Liverpool: Tate Publishing.

9 Henderson cited in Campany, ibid, p 52.

10 Howells, R (2002) Self Portrait: The Sense of Self in British Documentary Photography, *National Identities*, 4:2,101-118 accessed online at http://dx.doi.org/10.1080/14608940220143808 on

21/3/2012.

11 Prins cited in Parr, M & Badger G, (2004) *The Photobook: A History volume 1*, London: Phaidon Press p.7.

12 Ibid, page 7.

13 Ibid, page 8.

14 Ibid, page 7.

15 Ibid, page 11.

16 Streitberger, A (2010) Photography and the book – Introduction, *Image & Narrative*, Vol 11, No 4 (2010).

17 Ed Ruscha, cited in, Hatch, K (2005) "Something Else": Ed Ruscha's Photographic Books, in *October* 111, Winter 2005, pp 107-26.

18 Ibid.

Print/Screen: Current and Future Dissemination of the Self-Published Artist's Book

ADAM VERITY
School of Art and Design
University of Lincoln

As an artist working with photography, the idea of self-publication is increasingly enticing. Exhibiting can be highly rewarding, but it can also be very time-consuming and difficult to realise. The timeframe can be limiting also, as it can be months or even years before your work gets onto the walls. My first foray into self-publishing came in the form of exhibition catalogues. I produced laser printed booklets for use in the gallery, primarily to allow visitors to identify the work. Despite the fact that these catalogues were relatively crude in the way that they were printed and assembled, there was instant satisfaction in seeing my work in sequenced, printed form.

In 2010, I began tentatively researching the area, leading me to libraries, artist's book fairs, and, perhaps crucially, online spaces. It seemed that I had been missing out on not only a significant heritage, but also a great deal of current debate surrounding the artist's book. I had been aware of some of the key practitioners in this genre: Ed Ruscha, John Baldessari, Bernd and Hilla Becher *et al*. However, I found myself interested not just in what had come before, but what role new technologies might be having on the self-publication of photographic books in the era of the Kindle[1] and iPad[2].

This chapter presents an overview of the current and potential future dissemination of what I will refer to as the artist's book. I will focus on self-published books by artists rather than either monographs or those books produced by established publishing houses. The intention is not to offer comprehensive analysis, but instead to offer an outline of the landscape of self-publication in 2012, using the key examples of print-on-demand and screen-based publishing. I shall, therefore, be referring to a number of recent cultural and technological developments in order to point towards the novel and alternative modes of dissemination which may materialise. In *Remediation: Understanding New Media* Bolter and Grusin argue that "all currently active media (old and new, analog and digital) honor, acknowledge, appropriate, and implicitly or explicitly attack one another." [3]

Developing and emerging technologies clearly play a key role in the development of artistic practice. In the case of the artist's book, fast and cost-effective printing becoming readily available made the democratic multiple a possibility. Through the internet, portable electronic devices, and even virtual bookshops within Second Life[4], the potential for dissemination is vast, and yet the issue of archiving and collecting work remains as pertinent as ever.

Online repositories such as Flickr[5] and Facebook[6], allow the storage of our digital content and images, as well as fostering online communities of interest. This proliferation also gives artists a cause to reconsider the printed image. Images often remain confined to the digital realm, where they can easily be shared and distributed, rather than being printed commercially and stored in an album. However, while the online space may have provided something of a catalyst for people to once more embrace the printed image in the form of zines and artist's books, it also provides a key method of dissemination, with websites such as MagCloud[7], Lulu[8] and Blurb[9] offering a print-on-demand service. These services are increasingly sophisticated, offering digital-only purchases, print-on-demand, and also ISBN assignment. Sites such as Self Publish Be Happy[10] and Motto Distribution[11] provide a place to share and collect only physical, limited edition artist's books.

This amalgamation of the hand-made,

tangible book with the online space is potentially problematic ideologically, as the aesthetic and conceptual underpinnings of the artist's book seem to stem partially from a reaction against mass production and commercialisation. The ease of access then could be seen as opposing the movement's principles, where artists typically share work at book fairs, via mail order, or through independent bookshops. Perhaps the overriding issue with this online presence is that the digitisation also affects the notion of the limited edition, which in turn shifts emphasis away from the artist's book as a finite article.

Perhaps the various online spaces function as a means of propagating the artist's book community, rather than simply providing a substitution for it. Or should we be cautious about digitising the artist's book, as opposed to looking at this as an evolutionary step? With Amazon announcing that they are currently selling more digital than print copies[12], is the printed book in some way 'at risk'? Or is the use of these new media technologies simply part of an on going remediation?

To begin to address some of these questions, in *A Manifesto for the Book* Bodman and Sowden suggest that, "Many artists consider digital output via mobile phones, Internet, screen-based and e-books as a means of producing a democratic multiple, and are not necessarily concerned about monetary recompense, the longevity of the piece, or any archival possibility".[13] Certainly the ability to create and publish artists' books digitally, and disseminate them with the same ease as uploading content to Facebook will be an attractive prospect to some artists. In some ways the immediacy is perhaps the key impulse, taking precedence over aesthetic considerations for some. However, the issue of how these works may be archived is also relevant. If some artists are not necessarily concerned with how their work may be preserved, then who will step forward? Simply collating and storing a list of websites will not necessarily ensure that work is archived due to the transient nature of web hosting.[14] A few hours of general web research, even today, will most likely highlight several links to pages which no longer exist.

Dissemination and distribution

Companies such as Blurb and Lulu facilitate publications being stored online where they can be previewed, downloaded or printed on-demand. The era of artists storing short or medium-sized runs of their publications in their own home may have come to an end. There are limitations, of course, especially in terms of the level of customisation available, as well as quality control. Nevertheless, the options for online publication are impressive given the unit cost to both the artist and the collector.

In some respects self-publishing for specific devices such as Apple's iPad are less accessible than either print-on-demand, or online publication. Many of the web-based resources which allow the emulation of a book, complete with animated page turns (such as Issuu[15]), do not currently fully operate on the iPad as they use proprietary web protocols which are not yet supported. Whilst making a simple PDF document that is almost universally readable is a possibility, there is a need for more sophisticated authoring tools to take full advantage of tablets and eReaders. Interactivity and integration with hardware, for example, involve a level of programming that will likely fall outside the skillset of the majority of artists. There have been movements towards making this process more accessible, however. In January 2012, Apple announced a free software application: iBook Author[16], which facilitates the creation of books for publication to their own iBookstore. Despite the fact that work created with this software will only be readable on Apple devices, the artist will at least be able to control the way their work will be received, as well as take advantage of the vast network and powerful search engine to aid distribution.

Nieves[17] is a publishing house based in Zurich, Switzerland which has both an online shop for limited-edition printed work, and an iPad application, which allows the purchase of digital-only versions designed and formatted for the screen of that device. By offering work which was sold as a limited edition in print form, as a complete digital download, there is perhaps a subtle tension between the ethos of the two strands of the company. The design of the on-screen bookshop shows the zines in sealed plastic wrappers as they might appear in printed form. The simple animation and the layout of the screen-based offering feels like they are tentatively exploring the possibilities as a revenue stream, rather than necessarily taking advantage of what devices such as this could offer to the reader.

My personal collection of artists' books are spread between the shelves of my bookcase, the virtual bookcase of my iPad, and my laptop hard drive, along with bookmarks in my web browser. Other people would add to this: the virtual bookcase within their Second Life homes, for example. While discussion about the correct use of the term 'artist's book' in an ever-widening context continues, issues surround the collection and archiving of the wealth of digital and new media works are also part of ongoing discussion. In an interview with Maria White, the Chief Cataloguer at Tate Britain, Bodman and Sowden discovered that artists' books must at this time essentially be physically printed in order to become part of the Tate archive[18]. So unless a new approach to the collection and preservation of digital artists' books is developed, there could be many works which will be excluded from this important archive, and will potentially be lost. While researching, I found several non-working links within online sites which indicated that they contained archives of artists' books and online journals; this serves to highlight the importance of libraries, museums and special collections taking an increased interest in digital works which may otherwise be lost.

The future

The iPad, with its easily portable dimensions, is more closely aligned to the experience of the traditional book than most computer monitors or laptop screens. As well as being similar in form, and handheld, crucially it allows physical interactivity via touchscreen technology which makes for a different experience to that of using a conventional computer display. The device is more than a simple book reader, offering as it does several powerful functions, more commonly found on a laptop computer, and it is priced to reflect this functionality. As a means of experiencing the artist's book then, it is generally perhaps not aligned with the notion of the democratic multiple. The cost of devices such as this will inevitably change over time, challenging this position.

Kadir van Lohuizen's book *Via PanAm*[19] is an example of a project designed specifically for the iPad. Taking advantage of interactivity, touchscreen controls, moving image and sound, the book is also designed to be constantly updated via an internet connection. Van Lohuizen documented his 25,000 kilometre journey across the Americas by uploading content at regular intervals to create a vast bookwork in real time. Van Lohuizen has said that: "The idea is to investigate whether we can regain our independence as authors. I think that, financially, it could be feasible... If I pull it off, I guess it will be easier for other photographers to pitch their own projects".[20] The cost of just the initial setup and design of the book for the iPad was €35,000 so, as an early-adopter of this form of publication, artists and publishing companies will no doubt be interested in how financially successful the project becomes. These sorts of projects, which allow the artist to create an almost entirely new experience for the reader, will be very important to the future of digital publication, particularly for the iPad. Given that Apple takes a percentage of all sales from the iBookstore, it has a vested interest in supporting this type of experiment as the possibilities of digital publication widen.

The implications of such technological developments on the artist's book of the future is potentially vast. Despite some artists and organisations making firm decisions about the sphere in which they choose to exist, the progressive convergence between the book and modes of digital publication cultivate an emerging field of practice for those who wish to explore the territory. As Bolter and Grusin summarise: "New digital media are not external agents that come to disrupt an unsuspecting culture. They emerge from within cultural contexts, and they refashion other media, which are embedded in the same or similar contexts." [21] The latest version of the iPad released by Apple in March 2012 features a screen with 264 pixels per inch, which reportedly out-resolves the human eye at working distances. Alongside this, the electronic ink technology (which more closely resembles the look of paper, rather than a glowing backlit screen) and flexible screen technology are becoming increasingly sophisticated. Over the next several years we are likely to see rapid developments in consumer screen-based devices, and the possibilities of self-publication will expand along with them.

Despite the ongoing technological and cultural developments towards digital formats, platforms of production, and distribution and publication, the modes of production associated with the physical artist's book still flourish in today's media environment. As such, emerging forms of dissemination demonstrate a re-fashioning and re-appropriation of these established technologies and practices.

As a practitioner, I make use of analogue film and mechanical typewriters despite the fact that for some, the digital alternatives which exist offer more cost-effective and convenient results. Therefore, I feel that while digital developments can inform and influence art practice, the printed book will continue to be a key part of the activity, even if this is increasingly alongside alternative forms.

It is the territory between digital and analogue which offers both creative potential and, through such rapid progression and fluidity, challenges for those engaged with collection and preservation.

NOTES

1 Kindle is a digital eBook reader produced and sold by online retailer Amazon.com Inc.

2 iPad is a tablet computer produced and sold by Apple Inc.

3 Jay Davis Bolter and Richard Grusin, *Remediation: Understanding New Media* (London: MIT Press, 2000) 67.

4 Second Life is an online environment where users can navigate through a virtual world via avatars. http://secondlife.com/.

5 Flickr is a web site and online community where users upload digital images. http://www.flickr.com/.

6 Facebook is a highly popular online social network on which users frequently upload digital images. http://www.facebook.com/.

7 MagCloud is an online service which offers both digital sales and a print-on-demand service, operated by Hewlett-Packard Development Company, L.P.

8 Lulu is a popular print-on-demand service based in North Carolina, USA.

9 Blurb is a successful print-on-demand service based in California, USA. Their website contains the following statement: "there's no good reason why it should take tons of time, technical skills, big bucks, or friends in high places to publish a book. Or a zillion books, for that matter."

10 Self Publish Be Happy is an online community and retailer supporting the distribution of self-published works.

11 Motto Distribution is a distributor of magazines and fanzines which began in Switzerland.

12 "E-Books Outsell Print Books at Amazon." Last modified May 19, 2011. http://www.nytimes.com/2011/05/20/technology/20amazon.html.

13 Sarah Bodman and Tom Sowden, *A Manifesto for the Book: With an Edited Selection of Interviews, Essays and Case Studies* (Bristol: Impact Press, 2010) 8.

14 Ibid.

15 Issuu is an online service which allows the digital publication of magazines and books, and facilitates the embedding of this material online. It currently claims 52 Million readers online. http://issuu.com/about.

16 iBook Author is primarily aimed towards the creation of text books for educational purposes, however it could be used for the creation of other content. Crucially it allows the easy implementation of some of the powerful tools that the device has to offer.

17 Nieves is a publisher and online bookshop based in Switzerland, specialising in artists' books and zines.

18 Bodman and Sowden, *A Manifesto for the Book* 87-89.

19 *Via PanAm* is available only as an iPad application currently. Each time that it is opened, there is an option to download the latest content from the internet.

20 *British Journal of Photography Online*. "Photography on the iPad: The Road to Success?". Last modified Dec 19, 2011. http://www.bjp-online.com/british-journal-of-photography/report/2127267/photography-ipad-road-success.

21 Jay Davis Bolter and Richard Grusin, *Remediation: Understanding New Media* (London: MIT Press, 2000) 9.

Bibliography

Baldessari, John. *Brutus Killed Caesar.* Emily H. Davis Art Gallery of the University of Akron, 1976.

Bodman, Sarah. and Tom Sowden. *A Manifesto for the Book: With an Edited Selection of Interviews, Essays and Case Studies.* Bristol: Impact Press, 2010.

Bolter, Jay David., and Richard Grusin *Remediation: Understanding New Media.* Cambridge: MIT Press, 2000.

British Journal of Photography Online. "Photography on the iPad: The Road to Success?". Last modified Dec 19, 2011. http://www.bjp-online.com/british-journal-of-photography/report/2127267/photography-ipad-road-success. *British Journal of Photography.* Incisive Media, Last modified Jan 26, 2012. iPad Edition.

Drucker, Johanna., and Granary Books. *The Century of Artists' Books.* New York: Granary Books, 2004.

Ekdahl, Janis. "Artists' Books and Beyond: The Library of the Museum of Modern Art as a Curatorial and Research Resource." [In 0019-0217]. *Inspel* 33, no. 4 (1999 1999): 241-48.

Jenkins, Henry. *Convergence Culture: Where Old*

and New Media Collide. New York: New York University Press, 2006.

Klanten, Robert., Adeline Mollard, Matthias Hübner. *Behind the Zines: Self-Publishing Culture*. Die Gestalten Verlag, 2011.

LeWitt, Sol. *Photo Grids*. New York: Rizzoli, 1978.

Miles, Melissa. "The Drive to Archive: Conceptual Documentary Photobook Design." *Photographies* 3, no. 1 (2010/04/14 2010): 49-68.

Murray, Susan. "Digital Images, Photo-Sharing, and Our Shifting Notions of Everyday Aesthetics." *Journal of Visual Culture* 7, no. 2 (August 1, 2008 2008): 147-63.

New York Times. "E-Books Outsell Print Books at Amazon." Last modified May 19, 2011. http://www.nytimes.com/2011/05/20/technology/20amazon.html.

Ruscha, Edward. *Twentysix Gasoline Stations*. Alhambra: Cunningham Press, 1969.

Van Lohuizen, Kadir. *Via PanAm*, Stitching Paradox, Last modified Nov, 19 2011. iPad Edition.

Pictures of Things and Things that are Pictures

DAVID PENNY

Manchester Institute for Research and Innovation in Art and Design (MIRIAD)

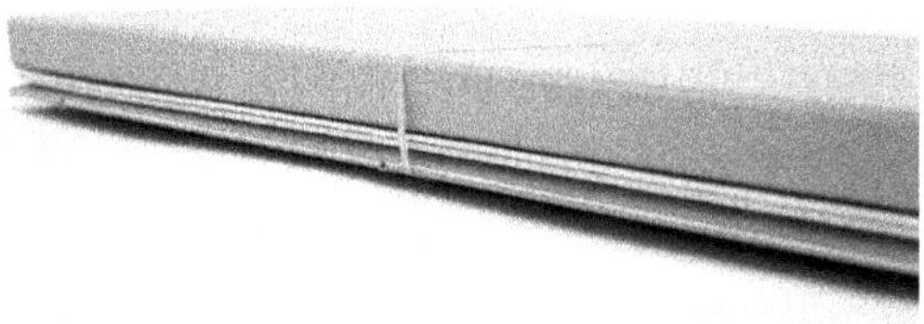

The final book...

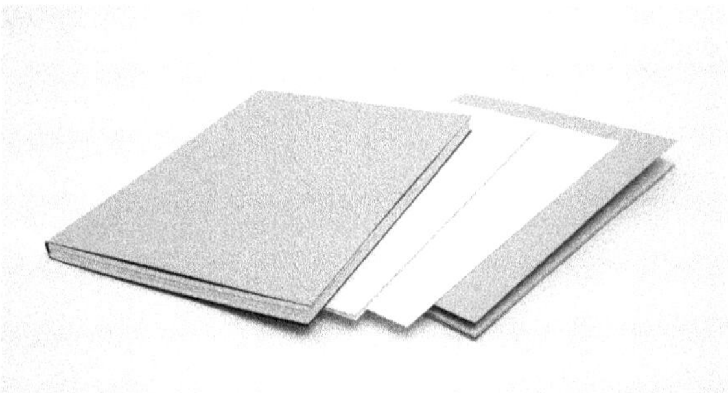

became a collection of pamphlets...

I could not simply start at the beginning with the first picture. The first picture might discount everything that has gone before, those other pictures I have made, the things I see in the street, fleeting thoughts I cannot grasp. To start in the middle would be better. Each contact print was trimmed and files were printed to an appropriate size, a normal practice for making such a document. But what next, where to put the first picture? [1]

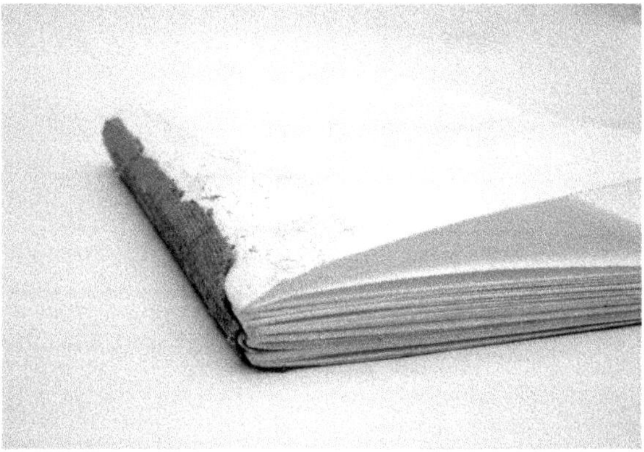

It was important that the construction of the book represented the process of making the images themselves.

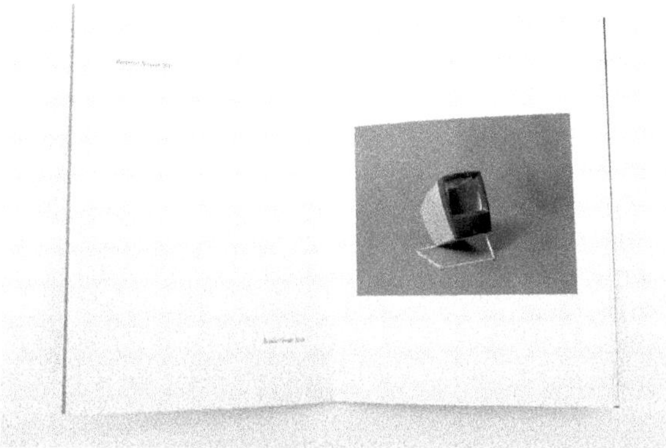

Allowing space to consider an image on its own

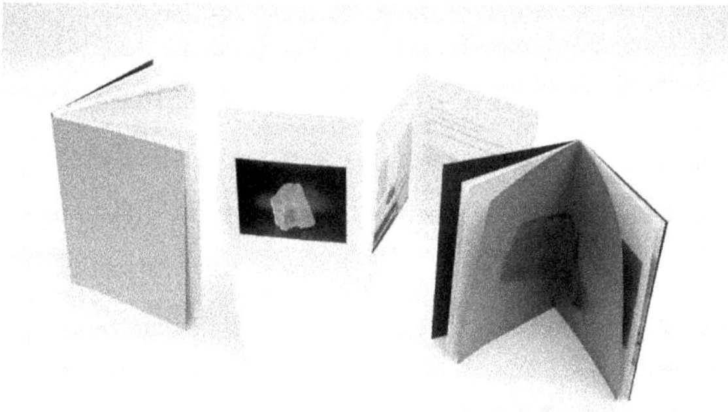

To invite a reading of the different series from page to page and section to section

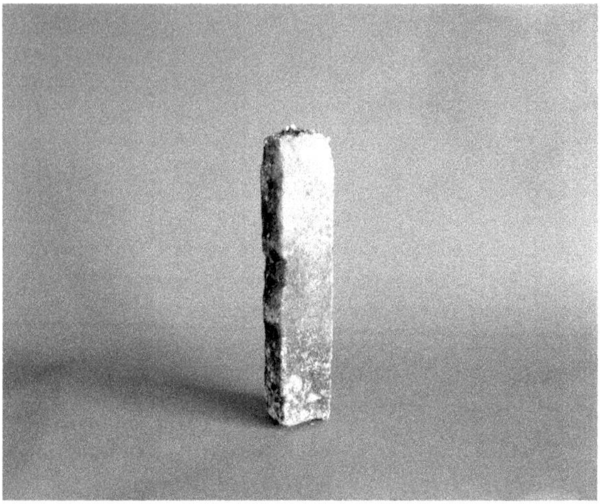

Totem *from the series* Outside of the Walls *(2011)*

The most elusive of images, those most in need of active interpretation or supplement, are often the ones that look the most plain or obvious. This is because there is never an absolute separation of the fantasy and reality either of images or of objects.[2]

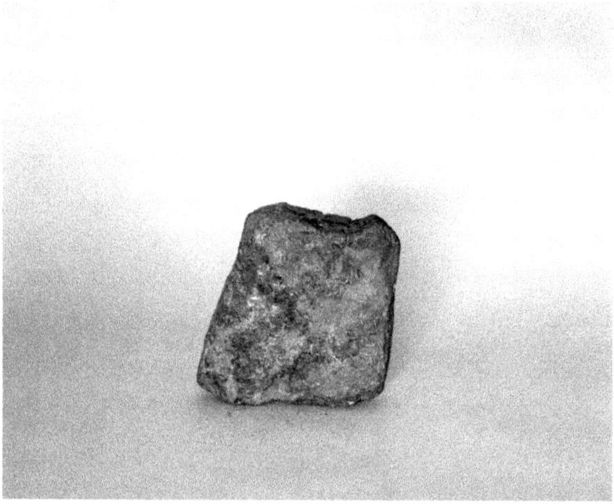

Shaft *from the series* Outside of the Walls *(2011)*

The series is no longer a "picture", and none of the canons of pictorial aesthetics can be applied to it. Here the separate picture loses its identity as such and becomes a detail of assembly, an essential structural element of the whole which is the thing itself. In this concatenation of its separate but inseparable parts, a photographic series inspired by a definite purpose can become at once the most potent weapon and the tenderest lyric.[3]

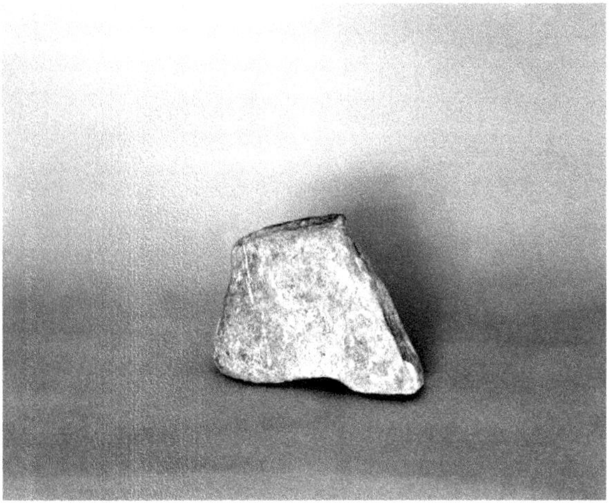

Proud *from the series* Outside of the Walls *(2011)*

A viewer is thus subtly spurred to try to interpret the series in non-meteorological, non-narrative ways and thus venture into the abstract or spiritual reflections Stieglitz hoped to inspire.[4]

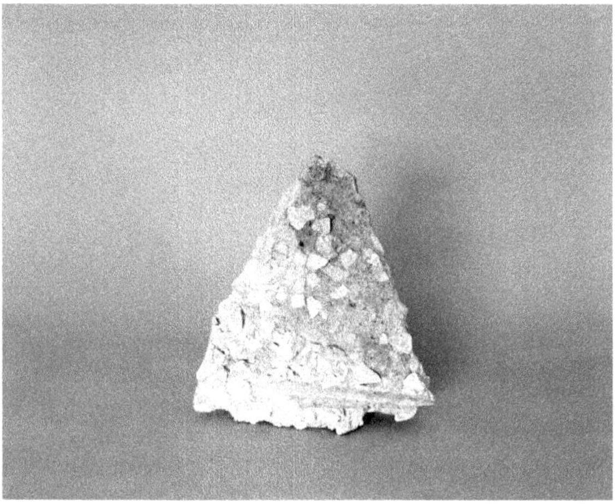

Point from the series Outside of the Walls *(2011)*

The artistic researcher acquires his or her own personal knowledge, constructed over time by way of social and cultural, embodied and cognitive experiences, only part of which is immediately expressible; much knowledge remains out of scope, present in the background of thought and action. Becoming aware of this background knowledge and practice can reveal interesting aspects, and so lead to new and rich research material, even if it also consigns us to constant wrestling with ideas that hover on the brink of crystallisation.[5]

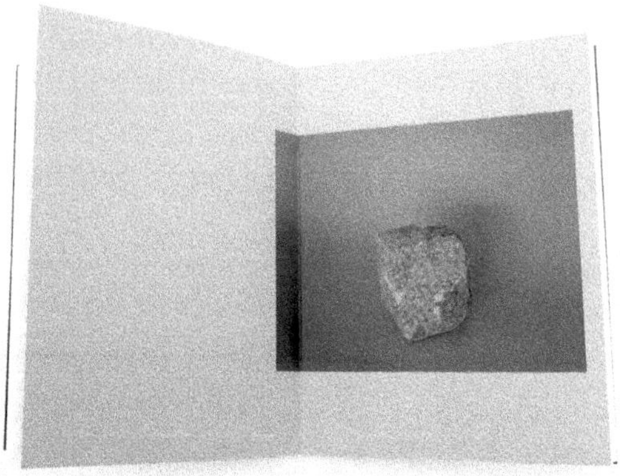

Perhaps finding resonance with another

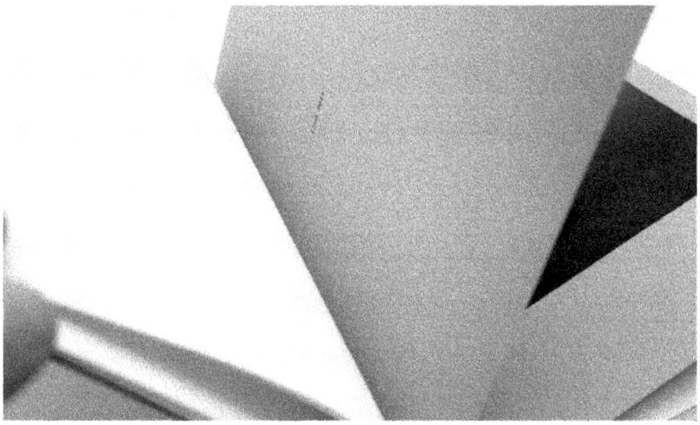

Echoes of paper stock as a motif of disparate series

I often wonder, I often wonder, I often wonder...
But that is just the point...[6]

NOTES

1 Thoughts on considering where to start, when making an artist's book.

2 Campany, D. 2004. Glass Camouflage: Photography, Objects and Objectivity. In: Seelig, T. & Stahel, U. (eds.) *The Ecstasy of Things: from the functional object to the fetish in 20th century photographs*. Göttingen ; [Great Britain]: Steidl. 266.

3 Moholy-Nagy, L. & Kostelanetz, R. 1970. *Moholy-Nagy*, [S.l.], Praeger. 54.

4 In reference to *Equivalents,* a sequence of five cloud scenes by Alfred Stieglitz. Smith, J. & Barberie, P. 2008. *More than one: photographs in sequence*, New Haven, Conn. ; London, Yale University Press. 13

5 Coessens, K., Crispin, D. & Douglas, A. 2009. *The Artistic Turn – A Manifesto*, Ghent, Orpheus Instituut. 71.

6 Some thoughts I arrived at whilst putting together this essay. The background intent of the wondering seems to have now been lost or forgotten as a product of the repetition.

Photographs, Notebooks, Interiority: Francesca Woodman's Artist's Books

JANE SIMON
Macquarie University
Sydney, Australia

This chapter considers the relationship between photography and the space of the artist's book through a close reading of Francesca Woodman's *Some Disordered Interior Geometries* (1981).

Some Disordered Interior Geometries uses a found notebook – an Italian geometry exercise book – to which Woodman has added her own photographs and handwritten text. Woodman's exploration of perception and photographic seeing is furthered by her use of the book page as an architectural surface and the book form as a three-dimensional space with a "disordered interior". Engaging with debates about the role of photography in the artist's book, this chapter positions *Some Disordered Interior Geometries* as a scaffold for exploring the flatness of photography and for thinking about interior space.

In 1986 a solo show of Woodman's work travelled to several American galleries. Since then there has been increasing critical attention given to Woodman's photographs and, according to Chris Townsend, "Since the mid-1980s Francesca Woodman has become one of the most talked about, studied and influential of contemporary photographers." [1] Woodman's body of work is largely composed of black and white photographs which mostly include representations of herself.

Woodman's photographs were made in the period of her life between age thirteen and twenty-two, the age of her death. Because of Woodman's early death and the accomplished and cohesive body of work she left behind, there has been a tendency in the critical responses to Woodman's photographs to focus on her status as a young photographic genius at the expense of engaging rigorously with her work. As Claire Raymond writes: "critical and cultural discomfort with the idea of a female prodigy is the engine that too often drives responses to Woodman's art." [2]

Many of Woodman's photographs contain representations (albeit often blurry ones) of herself. However, Woodman's project is not an autobiographical one. Recent work on Woodman emphasises her engagement with the conditions of photography, visibility and seeing, and her repetitive use of architectural frames.[3] Raymond, in *Francesca Woodman and the Kantian Sublime*, makes a convincing case that Woodman's self-portraits are an investigation of the nature of photography, space and perception, and are not an autobiographical project.[4] My own reading of Woodman's work takes seriously Woodman's investigation of space and photographic seeing, by focusing on the links between the space of the book and the space of the photographs. Despite Woodman's repetitive use of empty or derelict interiors, a focus on the (often crumbling) structures of buildings and, in the case of one of her later works, the *Temple Project*, printing on architectural paper, critics have largely sidestepped the question of architectural space in Woodman's work. Raymond's response to Woodman is an exception. Raymond highlights Woodman's "concern with architectonics",[5] and suggests that "[i]t is in that terrain of an architectonic theorization of perception that... Woodman intervenes."[6] While Woodman's body appears in various photographs amidst old churches, abandoned buildings and crumbling interiors, as Raymond puts it, "her figure is the figure of the viewer that ballasts the volatile, fragile architectural frame, and nothing else."[7] Further, as I have discussed elsewhere, Woodman uses her own figure or body as a space through which to think about the materiality of photography and to encourage viewers to observe the relationship of equivalence between bodies, object and interior spaces.[8] This continues in *Some Disordered Interior Geometries*. In her reading of *Some Disordered Interior Geometries* Johanna Drucker suggests that Woodman is showing us her self.[9] While Woodman certainly appears in the book (although it is typically a "covered" appearance with her head often cropped out of the frame or her hands covering her face), I suggest that the book is less focused on Woodman herself and more focused on the nature of photographic perception and the space of the book itself.

During her short career Woodman produced six artist's books. Five of these books were made using old notebooks and school exercise books that were printed in the early 1900s. The one book which doesn't use a found book as its base is *Portrait of a Reputation.*[10] That book consists of a small sequence of five images presented without any accompanying text on white pages. The first image begins with a portrait of Woodman wearing a black glove held up to her chest, and the final image is a photograph of black handprints on a flat surface. The book operates, Harriet Riches points out, as a flick book in which "Woodman's animated disappearance plays out the drama of the process of photographic self-representation as it hinges on the negative moment."[11] The book is sewn together in one corner with thin red ribbon, and the cover contains the handwritten title.

The other five books include *Angels, Calendar Notebook*, which uses a collection of poems, printed to appear handwritten and to which Woodman has attached her images and added her own handwritten text. *Quaderno dei Dettati e dei Temi* (*Notebook of Dictations and Compositions*) includes many of Woodman's well-known photographs such as *Self-Portrait at Thirteen* which have been printed onto transparencies or film and are taped onto pages which themselves are full of handwritten text in Italian. *Some Disordered Interior Geometries* similarly uses an aged Italian geometry exercise book – to which Woodman has added her black and white photographs and handwritten text. It was published in 1981 by Synapse Press, a small press in Philadelphia specialising in artist's books. The Synapse publication is a facsimile of the book.[12] More recently, Silvana Editoriale has posthumously published Francesca Woodman's *Notebook*, a direct facsimile of one of Woodman's artist's books that again uses an old Italian notebook as the background for a photographic narrative.[13] Woodman made these books in the late 1970s, and in the case of *Some Disordered Interior Geometries* in 1980-1981.

While Woodman's books can be situated as part of the flourishing interest in the photographic artist's book in the 1970s, Woodman's books resist any neat classification. They don't, as Harriet Riches points out in her discussion of *Portrait of A Reputation*, align with the deadpan and mass produced aesthetic of Ed Ruscha's books,[14] which are taken to be representative of the conceptual photographic artist's book in the 1970s. Woodman's artist's books combine narrative series, formal explorations of the book and of the photograph as well as a considered use of a hand-made aesthetic in her use of hand-written text and pasted on photographs and transparencies. While other artists were busy exploring the conceptual possibilities of the mass produced artist's book, Woodman's exploration of the book form combined an interest in the found-object (in the form of used exercise books) and a hand-made aesthetic.

Many of Woodman's photographs draw attention to the physical qualities of buildings, walls and floors. In Woodman's images wallpaper hangs off walls, surfaces appear to be crumbling, interiors are full of stains and accumulations of dust and dirt, floorboards are unpolished and full of texture, walls are cracked, paint is

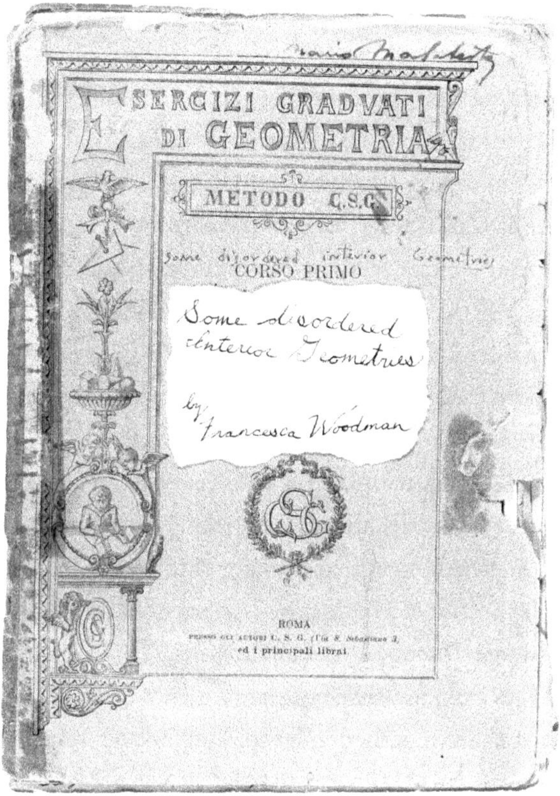

Francesca Woodman, cover Some Disordered Interior Geometries, *1980-1981, Courtesy George and Betty Woodman.*

chipped, doors are off their hinges and fireplaces are dismantled. Just like the architectural surfaces that Woodman is drawn to photograph, the found books that she uses as the basis for most of her artist's books are similarly used, decrepit and well-handled and, in the case of *Some Disordered Interior Geometries*, the pages include sections covered in correction fluid. Woodman seems to instinctively understand the book page as a sort of building site, echoing Anna Gibbs' description of the page as "never truly blank: always, on the contrary, already too heavily inscribed, a construction site filled with ruins and rubble." [15] Here Gibbs is making a point about the book page as a space which carries an automatic reference to other pages and other books. Woodman's use of found exercise books that are literally already inscribed, is an open acknowledgment that the page of the book – like the interior of a building – is a space of accretions.

Some Disordered Interior Geometries includes pages from multiple booklets which Woodman has joined together under the single cover with its original title *Esercizi Graduati di Geometria*.[16] Woodman's own title appears twice on the cover, directly on the purple cover in non-cursive handwriting, and again in cursive script within the torn paper addition to the cover. Woodman's script varies throughout, as Alison Dunhill notes, between a "mock early twentieth century joined copperplate" and her own "late twentieth

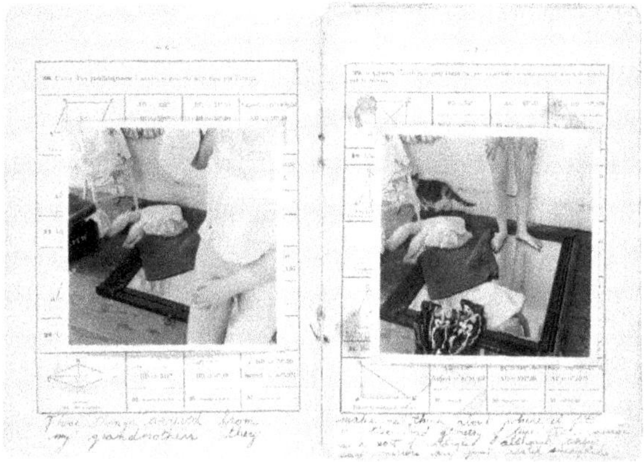

Francesca Woodman, pages from Some Disordered Interior Geometries, *1980-1981, Courtesy George and Betty Woodman.*

century hand script."[17] This shift in handwriting, along with the book's combination of an early twentieth century Italian text with photographs made in the late twentieth century points towards Woodman's concern not only with the geometry of space but also, to use Woodman's own phrase, "the odd geometry of time."

Toward the middle of *Some Disordered Interior Geometries*, two photographs are paired that show a mirror placed on the floor with clothes strewn over it. In the first image, Woodman appears perched in front of the mirror with her face cropped out of the frame, wearing a blouse and with her hand covering her naked bottom half. In the second image Woodman stands towards the back of the mirror, her hands splayed over her thighs, with a cat casually walking away from her. Her image is reflected in the mirror and is partly covered by the pile of clothing. Below the two images Woodman's annotation reads, "These things arrived from my grandmothers they make me think about where I fit in the odd geometry of time. The mirror is a sort of rectangle although they say mirrors are just water specified." Raymond interprets these images and Woodman's writing as being about the nature of female inheritance, with Woodman's phrasing a "frank assertion of the importance of female precursors and in its simultaneous poignant address of the problematic nature of female inheritance."[18] The clothes are given – passed down – but they don't necessarily clothe, or fit. Raymond also points out that the use of the word *odd* doesn't necessarily mean *strange*, but rather a geometric sense of the word: "*Odd geometry of time* means the point – the sharp point – of time, the place where time bends sharply, in the way that a line sharply bends at the point of an odd angle."[19]

Photography itself plays a "sharp" role in the movement of time, cutting a slice of a dynamic world and flattening it to the two-dimensional space of a photograph. Woodman's photography, as Townsend describes, works through the problem of the "gap, however small, between the interior geometry of the lens and the image and the exterior geometry of the world." [20] *Some Disordered Interior Geometries* examines this disparity between physical objects and two-dimensional photographs through its juxtaposition of a system of clear geometric explanations and symbols with photographs and annotations.

However, it also does this through the use of the book form – a three-dimensional physical object. The book itself, like the photograph, is another kind of framing device. Like a photograph the book page has a frame – the edges of the page. The book page also has its own spatial logic. As Nola Farman describes, writing about artist's books:

> *the page is a surface for inscription, a form for the moulding of light inviting a sculptural approach, a plane for implied depth as in a painting (the picture plane), and it is also an architectural space of structured dimensions contained by the shape of the book and the composition of its contents.*[21]

The pages of *Some Disordered Interior Geometries* are

worn, well-handled and have long lost their straight edges. They are rectangular, but don't have neat angles and squared precision. Thus the precision of geometry in the textbook is not only juxtaposed against the shapes and bodies within Woodman's photographs, but also against the worn page itself – the page may begin as a perfect rectangle but over time the shape of the page changes.

The precise angles and shapes in the diagrams in the geometry textbook are mimicked but not met in the shapes and angles Woodman produces in her photographs, which themselves are all square prints. In one photograph a hand lies atop a stool. Across the palm of the hand lies a white glove – a recurring motif in Woodman's work. At the bottom of the page, Woodman has drawn an incomplete circle that closely matches the size of the stool. On the opposite page, Woodman has translated the title of the book section, "problems to resolve: the surface area of triangles and parallelograms." In the photograph, Woodman seem to turn the three main objects – stool, hand, glove – into flat surface areas. There is no background, the stool seems to sit in darkness, the hand is stretched with a flat palm, and the glove lies flatly on top of the hand. And while

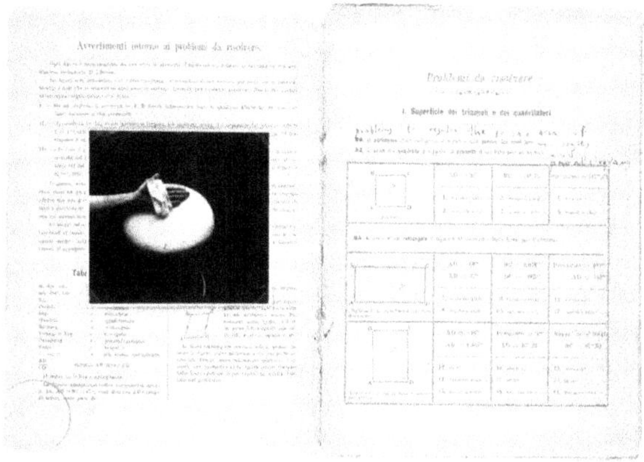

Francesca Woodman, pages from Some Disordered Interior Geometries, *1980-1981, Courtesy George and Betty Woodman.*

there are no true triangles or parallelograms in the photograph, the hand and glove together work to mimic a triangle and one starts to see the formation of four-sided shapes in the stretch of lower arm and the straightened fingers.

On another page of *Some Disordered Interior Geometries* is a photograph of a large seashell on a window sill. A hand reaches into the frame holding a rectangular piece of glass next to the shell. Beneath the photograph the text states "another rectangle". The piece of glass is rectangular, but so too is the window whose frame is weather-beaten and whose glass is splattered, and of course once you start looking for rectangles more and more

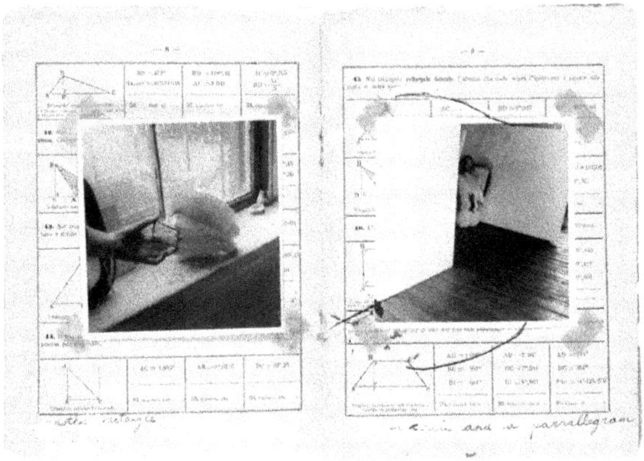

Francesca Woodman, pages from Some Disordered Interior Geometries, *1980-1981, Courtesy George and Betty Woodman.*

appear making the handwritten text as Dunhill notes, a "humorous understatement".[22] On the opposite page is an image of Woodman sitting on the floor with her back to the viewer, holding an unidentifiable object behind her curved naked back. She sits between two adjacent wall panels, one which is smudged and has a curved line across it. Following the curve Woodman has continued this line by drawing – wonkily – on the page beyond the frame of the photograph. She also extends the line of the bottom edge of one of the wall panels. Underneath this image the text states "a circle and a parrallegram" [sic]. On both pages text – perhaps written by the original user of the

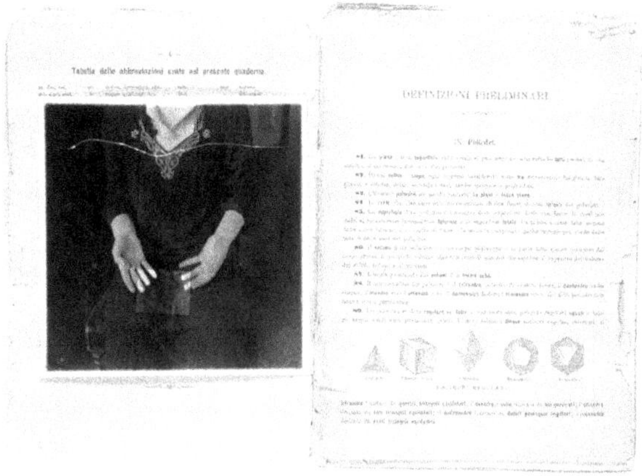

Francesca Woodman, pages from Some Disordered Interior Geometries, *1980-1981, Courtesy George and Betty Woodman.*

textbook – has been painted over with correction fluid, and written over by Woodman's text. The effect of this is to create more shapes on the page, but nebulous ones which contrast against the neat grids and shapes on the textbook page.

The first and the final photograph in *Some Disordered Interior Geometries* work as a sequence to bookend the concerns of the other pages. In both photographs, we see Woodman's seated torso, wearing dark clothing that merges her into the background of the image. Her hands, palms facing upwards, appear to hold a glass square under which her fingers appear lighter, almost glowing. The glass square works as yet another frame within

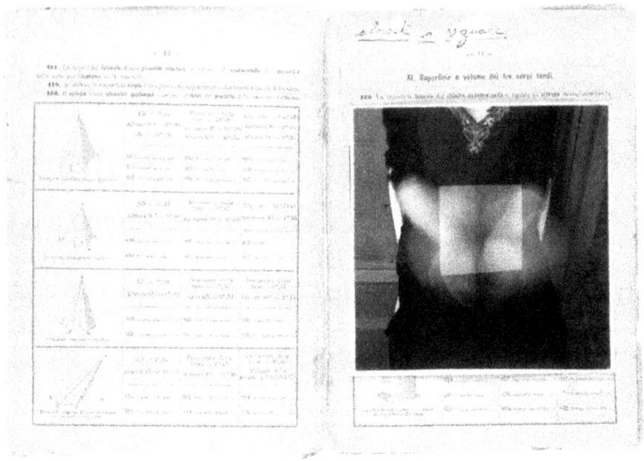

Francesca Woodman, pages from Some Disordered Interior Geometries, *1980-1981, Courtesy George and Betty Woodman.*

the frame of the photograph. On the opposite page are diagrams of a cube, an octahedron and other solid geometric shapes. In the final image of the book, the photograph has Woodman in the same clothing and position within the frame. This time her hands appear in movement, again beneath an uneven square shape. Above the photograph Woodman has written "almost a square".

The use of glass, and reference to framing devices is common in Woodman's work. *Space*^{2}, for example, is a series that features a glass museum case with Woodman's body contained, pressed up against, and spilling out of the glass case.[23] In the related *Study for Space*^{2}, Woodman again considers the formal constraints of photography, and in a similar manner to her hand-drawn shapes in *Some Disordered Interior Geometries* she draws frames around the distorted moving body which appear in each frame of the contact sheet. As I've noted elsewhere, it is important that Woodman refers to mathematical squaring rather than cubing. Squaring is two-dimensional and is a metaphor for the flat representation of space in a photograph.[24]

The clarity of the square glass pane in the opening image has lost its clear edges by the final image. Here it is *almost* a square; it is a square that is dissolving and is one of Woodman's many frames which challenge geometry's stability or coherence.[25] Other pages refer to the gap between the shapes of the interior space and the body within the space and the precise shapes of geometry. In one photograph, in which Woodman stands with her hands covering her face in front of a rough square of material pinned on a wall, she again writes "almost a square". In the second image of the book, Woodman again covers her face with her hand and her open mouth holds a round object. Underneath the photograph the text declares, "I a sort of round". If Woodman tries to simulate geometric shapes, they are imperfect: *almost* a shape or a *sort of* shape.

The stillness of the first image, with its in-focus glass square over Woodman's hands, has disappeared by the closing image. Photography stills space, and geometry is a neat system of classification, but for Woodman it is important to notice the disorder between what appears in the photographic frame and what falls away or gets lost in photographic representation.

According to Keith Smith, "the space of the page speaks aside from the content." [26] In artists' books, the page is not only a background for content. For a photobook to be considered an artist's book there needs to be some engagement with the form of the book – a thinking through of how a series of photographs is received in book form. *Some Disordered Interior Geometries* is messy in its presentation. It contains correction fluid over text, wonky-edged photographs and multiple styles of handwriting. This unpolished aesthetic fits with the conceptual point of the book – to see how interior spaces and bodies meet up with the flat plane of the photograph and the precision of mathematics. The book form itself – a decaying, well-handled object – echoes Woodman's interior surfaces – splattered windows, chipped surfaces, lived-in spaces. Just as the shapes within Woodman's photographs reach for – and fail to meet – geometric precision, the shape of the pages are *almost a rectangle* but are too worn to echo the straight lines of the diagrams contained within. *Some Disordered Interior Geometries* is a book about planes and volumes, photography and space, that uses the architecture of the book not as a container but as one of the forms with which Woodman poses a response to interior geometries.

NOTES

1 Chris Townsend, *Francesca Woodman: Scattered in Space and Time* (London: Phaidon, 2006), 6.

2 Claire Raymond, *Francesca Woodman and the Kantian Sublime* (Farnham: Ashgate, 2010), 13.

3 Raymond, 136.

4 Raymond, 1-20.

5 Raymond, 41.

6 Raymond, 4.

7 Raymond, 60.

8 Jane Simon, "An intimate mode of looking: Francesca Woodman's photographs," *Emotion, Space and Society*, Special Issue Researching intimate Spaces, 3 (2010): 28.

9 Johanna Drucker, *A Century of Artists' Books* (New York: Granary Books, 1995): 340.

10 For a detailed discussion of this book see Harriet Riches, "A Disappearing Act: Francesca Woodman's *Portrait of a Reputation*," *Oxford Art Journal* 27:1 (2004).

11 Riches, 112.

12 My discussion refers to the original source text of *Some Disordered Interior Geometries*, rather than the Synapse publication which, due to printing quality, doesn't capture Woodman's sculptural use of the book page in her layering in photographs over the base page. For an early review of the Synapse publication see Martha Gever, "Artists' Books: Alternative Space or Precious Object?" *Afterimage* (1982): 6-8.

13 Francesca Woodman, *Francesca Woodman's Notebook* (Milano: Silvana Editoriale, 2011).

14 In her discussion of *Portrait of a Reputation*, Riches points out that, 'Woodman's subject matter, along with the hand-made card cover and hand-scripted title inscribe this book with elements of her own subjectivity, introducing an element of selfhood seemingly at odds with the ostensibly "deadpan" subject matter and anti-literary form exemplified by Ruscha's gas stations,' 109.

15 Anna Gibbs cited in Nola Farman, *The Humours of the Artists' Book*, (PhD diss., University of Western Sydney, 2007): 173.

16 Alison Dunhill, "Dialogues with Diagrams: Francesca Woodman's book, some disordered interior Geometries," *Rebus* 2 (2008): 3.

17 Dunhill, 5.

18 Raymond, 37.

19 Raymond, 39.

20 Townsend, 50.

21 Farman, 11.

22 Dunhill, 23.

23 For a discussion of *Space*^{2}, see Rosalind Krauss, *Bachelors* (Cambridge, Mass: MIT Press, 1999): 162-165.

24 Simon, 32.

25 Raymond, 49.

26 Keith Smith, "The Book as a Physical Object" in *A Book of the Book*, ed. Jerome Rothenberg and Steven Clay (New York: Granary Books, 2000), 54-70.

Bibliography

Drucker, Johanna. *A Century of Artists' Books*. New York: Granary Books, 1995.

Dunhill, Alison. "Dialogues with Diagrams: Francesca Woodman's book, some disordered interior Geometries." *Rebus* 2 (2008): 1-32.

Farman, Nola. *The Humours of the Artists' Book*. unpublished PhD, University of Western Sydney, 2007.

Gever, Martha. "Artists' Books: Alternative Space or Precious Object?" *Afterimage* (1982): 6-8.

Krauss, Rosalind. *Bachelors*. Cambridge, Mass: MIT Press, 1999.

Raymond, Claire. *Francesca Woodman and the Kantian Sublime*. Farnham: Ashgate, 2010.

Simon, Jane. "An intimate mode of looking: Francesca Woodman's Photographs." *Emotion, Space and Society*, Special Issue Researching Intimate Spaces, 3 (2010): 28-35.

Smith, Keith. "The Book as a Physical Object." In *A Book of the Book*, edited by Jerome Rothenberg and Steven Clay, 54-70. New York: Granary Books, 2000.

Townsend, Chris. Francesca Woodman: *Scattered in Space and Time*. London: Phaidon, 2006.

Woodman, Francesca. *Some Disordered Interior Geometries*. Philadelphia: Synapse, 1981.
Woodman, Francesca. *Francesca Woodman's Notebook*. Milano: Silvana Editoriale, 2011.

Artists' Interventions in the Family Album

LOGAN SISLEY
Dublin City Gallery
The Hugh Lane

This chapter considers several artists' books that use the conventions of the pre-digital, family photograph album. As photography and book-making are brought together in the tradition of the family album, it offers fertile ground for artists' book projects. The majority of the works discussed in this essay use "found" – or "lost" – photographs, collected in various ways. While the conventions of the album privilege certain stories, the artists under consideration have altered the conventional relationship between image and narrative.

Divorced from the original context of their making and circulation, the photographs are open to new meanings. The main works discussed are *FLOH* by Tacita Dean, Fiona Tan's *Vox Populi* series, and the ongoing work of documentation céline duval, with reference to works by Christian Boltanski and Mohini Chandra.

While the projects share a strategy of re-using family photographs, they do so with different emphases that reflect ongoing concerns of the respective artists: Dean's interest in the recovery of analogue media in an increasingly digital age, Tan's focus on portraiture and identity, and Duval's interest in the circulation of photographic imagery. With the exception of Boltanski, the artists were all born in the 1960s and 70s and grew up in a period when making albums was a widespread practice, prior to being superseded by digital media.

When discussing these books, it is useful to make some general comments about the structure of the family album. This applies to the period following the mass availability of the camera in the home (in industrialised countries) and predating the rise of digital technology – in effect the second half of the twentieth century.

The family album falls within the wider practice of family photography, which refers both to the subject matter – photographs of family members – and to the context in which these photographs are produced and consumed.

Typically the photographs that comprise the family album are taken by a family member or a member of the family's social circle in the context of the life of the family. All the book projects discussed here take the photographs out of that context and circulate them in a wider public sphere.

While the context may be the domestic, a feature of family albums is that they do not, as a rule, document the mundane or everyday.

Rather, defining moments in the course of the family's life are chosen to be commemorated. Daily events are not, on the whole, deemed worthy of commemoration.[1] However, the first day at a new job, or the first day at school, or a meal marking a special event, such as a birthday, may well be included. Philip Stokes has identified several prominent motifs in the family album, based on research in England: the family standing outside the house, the garden archway, the family motorcar, and most of all, children and their games.[2] Dave Kenyon also notes the overwhelming presence of babies, various rites of passage, important possessions, hobbies, official photos and pets.[3] Christmases, holidays and weddings are all themes that are frequently incorporated, and which may also form standalone albums. Kenyon writes that family photography celebrates success, so it is not surprising then that the only major family gathering excluded from the album is the funeral, as it marks the reduction and impoverishment of the group.[4] There are exceptions and variations to these practices, which can be traced within the book projects discussed below, but the intent here is to simply provide a general framework for understanding the structure of the family album as a point of reference.

In celebrating success, the album is structured to demonstrate not only a narrative of the passing of time, but of the family's improvement over time. Many of the recurrent subjects – the home, the car, and the garden – are material indicators of social status – and photographs of these objects can be used to indicate increasing prosperity.

In Christian Boltanski's *Album de photos de la famille D., 1939-1964* (1972) the artist was frustrated in attempting to create a progressive chronological narrative. Initially presented as an exhibition at *Documenta* in 1972 and later realised in book form,[5] the work comprised a selection of photographs copied from the albums of Michel Durand-Dessert and arranged in an order that Boltanski determined to be chronological. Boltanski's attempt to reconstruct the lives of another family proved impossible. He realised "that these images were only witnesses to a collective ritual. They didn't teach us anything about the Family D... but only sent us back to our own past." [6]

Boltanski's first intervention in the family album came in 1969 with the photocopied book, *Recherche et présentation de tout ce qui reste de mon enfance, 1944-1950 (Research and presentation of everything that remains from my childhood, 1944-1950)* which was distributed as mail art. This autobiographical project included snapshots of family outings, a 1951 class portrait, photographs of childhood objects, and a page from a school essay. Boltanski described it as a "search for a part of myself that had died away, an archaeological inquiry into the deepest reaches of my memory." [7] However, most of the objects and images included were not his own, but his nephew's, questioning the nature of the authenticity of such archival records.

While family photography records certain things according to convention, many images are excluded. Patricia Holland asserts that family albums are about forgetting as well as remembering.[8] Or, as Annette Kuhn points out, family secrets are the other side of the family's public face.[9] Lurking behind this mask is a myriad of secrets, stories, problems, joys, and emotions that the conventions of the album are incapable of recording, except obliquely.

Even when prosperity is absent, the happy times, or the appearance of them, are emphasised. Anne Higonnet writes that the unspoken rules of photographing children result in there being "no tantrums, tears, or bruises, no mess, no pleading, no failures, no conflicts, no resistance, few if any expressions except smile."[10] The compulsion to smile for the camera is strong and the family album generally presents a happy face to the world. The camera may capture images of resistance – a hand raised to shield the face, a head turned to avoid the camera's gaze – but these are likely to be edited out of the family album. In this sense the album is doubly mediated. A first selection process takes place before the camera clicks, the second when the album is collated. Simon Watney sees the function of domestic photography as cohesion. It aims to "impart the semblance of retrospective coherence to family life, usually more or less chaotic and unpredictable."[11] The artists discussed below disrupt that cohesion and celebrate the chaotic and unpredictable.

The question of inclusion and exclusion is present in Tacita Dean's *FLOH*, produced in collaboration with Martyn Ridgewell.[12] The book comprises family photographs that Dean collected over a number of years in flea markets in Europe and America (*Floh* being the German word for *flea*).

In his comprehensive analysis of the book in the

journal *October*, Mark Godfrey states that because of the diversity of photographic subject matter he prefers "not to think of *FLOH* as a kind of collective photo album." [13] One of the reasons for this is that Dean deliberately includes "the mistaken photographs" (i.e. those that are out-of-focus or poorly framed) that are generally excluded in the selection process for compiling a family album.[14] He also notes that this is what marks the images in the book as pre-digital: "Digitalization discourages people from saving or printing out 'mistaken' photographs – they can be erased from a camera's memory before they have physical presence, erased without any superstitious misgivings." [15] Attention to the place of analogue technologies within the dominance of digital media is found in much of Dean's work. She has written that the digital world "just does not have the means to create poetry; it neither breathes nor wobbles, but tidies up our society, correcting it and then leaves no trace." [16]

Notwithstanding Godfrey's observation on Dean's inclusion of "bad" photographs, *FLOH* nonetheless remains "in effect an album." [17] The album-effect is heightened by the physical properties of the book – its cloth-bound hard cover in keeping with the traditional family album. It was sold in a slipcase with the publication details affixed to the front. The title was embossed on the front cover – the only text in the book apart from the artist's signature. This absence of printed text adds to the resemblance to the family album. That resemblance is broken, however, by the inclusion of full bleed images (some are double page spreads) which disrupts the illusion of photographs stuck on a page.

As the reader turns the pages of the book it becomes apparent that the images do not come from a coherent time or place, and apart from a few distinct groups of images, the same faces are not repeated throughout the album as might be expected. There is none of the progressive family narrative, but rather a series of chance encounters and juxtapositions, consistent with Dean's method of collecting the images in markets.

While an album primarily records a collective narrative – that of a family group – it also offers a means of structuring the past for individual members of that group. The life of the album depends on the continued relationship with a member of the family in which it was produced, a person who can identify the faces and places, and retell the associated stories. This contextual information will frequently slip away with the death of a relative. Richard Chalfen writes that: "no one sees your snapshots like you see them, and, in turn, you can't possibly see other collections quite like their custodians do." [18] Different members of the same family, with similar claims to the album, may view the images very differently.

Dean does not attempt to create a new narrative from the images. With other works she has published accompanying texts (termed *asides*) but not with *FLOH*. She did, however, produce a short text for a 2003 exhibition catalogue in which she wrote: "I do not want to give these images explanations: descriptions by the finder about how and where they were found, or guesses as to what stories they might or might not tell. I want them to keep the silence of the flea market; the silence they had when I found them; the silence of the lost object." [19] This places the responsibility on viewers to make connections between the images – or not.

The photographs exist collectively outside of the book as one of Dean's collections (others include four – and more – leaf clovers, and postcards of frozen fountains). Dean has remarked that, "Now I have resolved to believe that there is no, and can never be, a final version to this collection; that *FLOH* exists in the continuum and will one day, I hope, return, ownerless and silent to its origins in the flea market."[20] This sense of continuum evokes the notion of flow, as does the book's title, since the German *Floh* (*flea*) has the same pronunciation as the English *flow*.

Michael Newman describes Dean's approach to collecting as "concerned with the unrealised redemptive possibility contained in the object, which is generally an object that has fallen away from utility, which has become unmoored from the ship of progress, which is, one way or another, obsolete. Collecting, understood in this way, is akin to rescuing."[21]

Godfrey notes that all the photographs have in common "the fact of survival."[22] The lost photographs have found a new home – at least for the time being – with Dean. While she may not understand the images in the same way as their original owners, she nonetheless accepts a duty of care. A new personal relationship to each of the images is created. By signing and numbering every copy of the edition of 4000, she reinforces the sense that there is someone personally connected to the production of this book. Dean has also exhibited individual photographs under her name, extending her claim to the images.[23]

While Dean does not edit the photographic image – such as cleaning the surface or erasing any creases – she does crop the images to neat rectangles. The material qualities of the printed photograph are given greater emphasis in Mohini Chandra's book, *Album Pacifica*, also published in 2001.[24] The book features 100 photographs that Chandra collected of her family, reuniting a family which is dispersed across the globe. However, the artist only shows the backs of the photographs. The viewer doesn't see faces but only blank surfaces, photographer's marks, or notes identifying the time, place or people depicted. These details become clues to what might be there on the other side of the photographic paper, and remind us of the limitations of both the written and the visual in constructing histories. The artist says, "While the viewer is denied the actual photograph, they are able to conjure up an 'imaginary' photographic landscape... the work evokes a space in which the audience's own histories and experiences can be imagined,"[25] reminiscent of Boltanski's remark that viewing another person's album returns the viewer to his or her own histories.

Fiona Tan's series, *Vox Populi*, takes the

family photograph into a wider sphere. The first work in the series was made in Norway in response to a commission from the Norwegian parliament. Tan was struck by the portraits of members of parliament lining the corridors of the parliament building, commenting, "by running through the passages and hallways you could run through history." [26] She sought to make an alternative portrait of the nation to hang within the institution's walls, and set about identifying a wide group of possible contributors by word-of-mouth. Collecting stations were set up around the country, mostly in art museums, and Tan sifted through the images offered. She did not meet any of the photographs' owners at this stage, although they are all credited in the subsequent publications; the selection was made on her subjective response to the images alone. Asked what she was looking for in the images, she replied, "I don't think I can actually capture it in words. I know I was looking for the sorts of images you can only find in photo albums made by amateurs because they are so intimate and private." [27] In her own editing process she rejected certain types of professional photographs, such as class portraits or wedding shots, which do make their way into family albums. A total of 267 photographs were scanned, printed, framed and installed on the walls of the parliament building. These were then edited for publication. [28]

Three subsequent works followed, all using the same methodology: in Sydney, 301 photographs were exhibited at the Sydney Biennale of 2006, while 305 photographs made up *Vox Populi: Tokyo* in 2007, and *Switzerland* was first shown at the Aargauer Kunsthaus in 2010. All exhibitions have been followed by a publication. The final project, *Vox Populi: London*, is scheduled for exhibition and publication in 2012.

Rachel Kent's assertion that *Vox Populi: Sydney* "stands somewhat in contrast to the apparent visual homogeneity of the former work [Norway]..." [29] reflects how the identification of place prompts a different way of viewing the images to those encountered in *FLOH*, in which no contextual information is provided. In each of them, the viewer can perceive signs (or stereotypes) of the location – snow in Norway, the Sydney Opera House, cows in Swiss mountain fields, cherry blossom in Japan. There is also a narrower time span than in *FLOH* and all of the images chosen are in colour. While identifying a face within

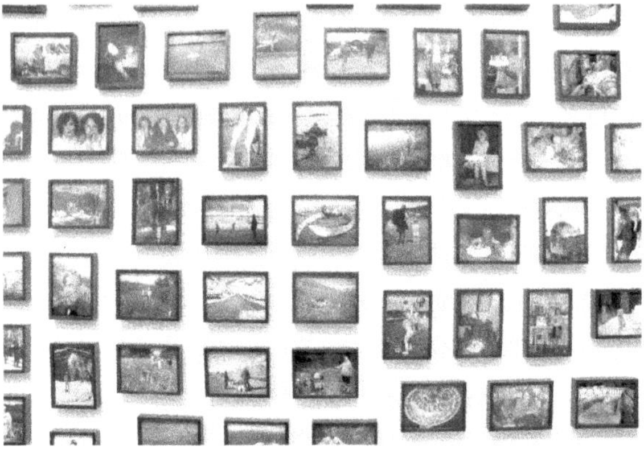

Fiona Tan, Vox Populi, Norway, *photographic installation, 2004. Courtesy the artist and Frith Street Gallery, London.*

305 photographs from a city of over 35 million inhabitants may be unlikely, the anticipation of potential recognition affects how actively local viewers might engage with the photographs.

The selected photographs stand in for a larger group, as the photographs in the Norwegian Parliament stand in for the people of Norway. The installed works operate as a mass portrait arranged in what Kent calls "informal groupings of photographs in serendipitous masses across the gallery wall."[30] To extend the earlier analogy, Dean's flow has become a flood of images that Tan then contains. The artist was surprised at the variety in the photographs, having been

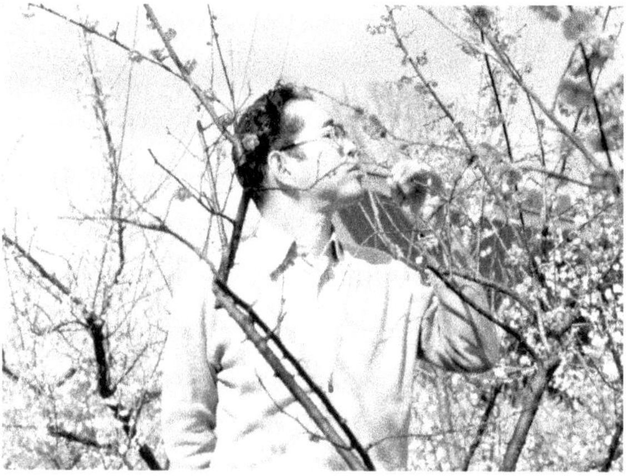

Fiona Tan, Vox Populi, Tokyo, *photographic installation, 2007. Courtesy the artist, Wako Works of Art, Tokyo and Frith Street Gallery, London.*

worried that she would get too much repetition. She later remarked that she learnt that "everyone takes photographs in a very distinct style and that no two Christmases are the same." [31] For all the conventions and exclusions described earlier, family photography offers endless variety within the seemingly endless repetition.

Each collection of images is accompanied by a commissioned essay. Kent notes in the Sydney edition that, "Scanning the flow of imagery, individual or family histories may also be mapped out from pregnancy to childhood and maturity." [32] The notion of flow, evocative of Dean's book, appears twice in Kent's text. Also echoing

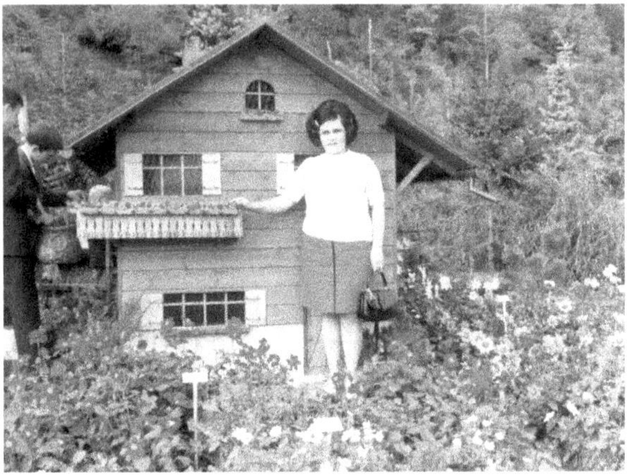

Fiona Tan, Vox Populi, Switzerland, *photographic installation, 2010. Courtesy the artist and Frith Street Gallery, London.*

Dean's thoughts on the silence of the images, she writes, "the *VOX POPULI* works are silent, the images 'speaking' for themselves through individual placement, selective groupings, drifts and flows of imagery that form a language built upon perception and identification." [33]

The fact that family photographs are frequently referenced in terms of speech or silence reveals their close relationship to storytelling. Tan herself has called the work "a noisy piece." She has remarked: "I remember some of the notes I wrote while I was hanging the piece on the wall and figuring it out in my studio. One day I wrote *This is a very noisy piece.* What I meant with that is that all the images are shouting to be seen. I started to think of these photos as individual voices then. Of course the title *Vox Populi* became then even more fitting." [34] The term *vox populi*, which literally means voice of the people, is often used on television and radio for interviews with members of the "general public". The intended effect is to provide a veneer of democratic access to media. Vernacular photography might offer the promise of the truth of the people, but like official portraiture, family photography is bound by rules and conventions, and Tan's exhibitions and books are mediated through the editing process.

While the installed photographs are all printed in a uniform size (13cm x 18cm), the images are reproduced in the books at varying scales (up to the page size of 12.6cm x 17.8cm). Photographs are grouped (e.g. parties or children at school) and the eye can drift from one to another. In each of the books they are divided into three categories: portraits, home and nature. The images are therefore classified in the books both by location and by these other categories determined by Tan, mimicking a sociological study. Suzanne Cotter calls this "quasi-ethnography." [35] She continues, "Although she has indicated the general classification system which structures *VOX POPULI, Norway* and essentially marks the passage from birth to death across time and seasons, Tan's digital archive of snapshots are evidence of other registers of order which are not openly declared in the work. A playful system of cross-references develops."[36]

Playful cross-references also operate in the work of documentation céline duval. Since the late 1990s, Céline Duval has been collecting photos: amateur snapshots, postcards, photos cut out from magazines, as well as her own pictures, and making works under the name documentation céline duval. She adopts a range of collecting practices, which she says was triggered initially by a type of voyeurism:

> *I started out buying snapshots at flea markets... then on the internet. Others are sent to me by friends, or else since two years now, I set up "encounters with your family albums", organized by various art centres, where I select photos in the albums of the participants. I scan them and return them to their owners with a CD of the scans and ask them to sign a transfer of right contract for the photos they lent. The collected pictures tend therefore to be more contemporary. The owners are informed of every*

> *publication I make and receive one or several copies of it. I can more easily fill in the gaps in my archives with the entire albums of the lenders. This databank is digital and therefore adds to my paper archives."*[37] *[She files] the next set of themes in gestations, the images which attract you, touch you and you don't yet know why. Sometimes it takes me over a year to understand."*[38]

From these collected images, documentation céline duval has produced a multitude of publications including *Cahier d'images – album de famille*, one of several collaborations with Hans Peter Feldmann (2001), and *La revue en 4 images*, which was produced in 60 editions. As the name suggests each edition comprised four images (although sometimes more and sometimes less). The images are frequently combined according to formal similarities or analogies, often in playful ways.

Unlike the previous works discussed, in which the images remain more or less "intact", those in *La revue en 4 images* are retouched and cropped, and reproduced in black and white. François Coadou writes: "The preparation of each of her photos involves minute corrections such as reframing and retouching with no reverence for the document.

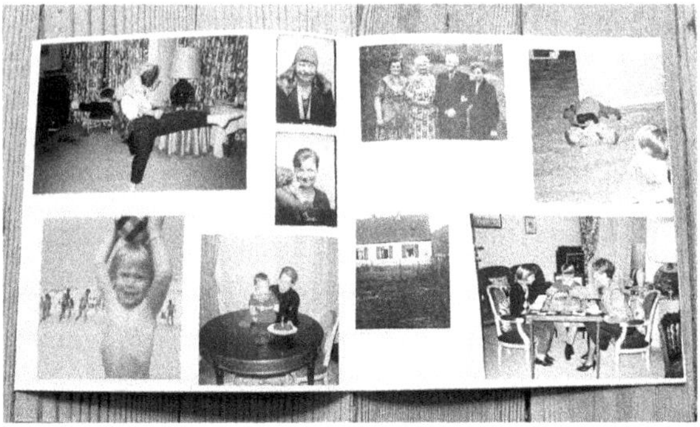

documentation céline duval & Hans Peter Feldmann, cahier d'images - album de famille, *feldmann verlag, Düsseldorf, 2001/11. Courtesy of the artists.*

This clears up the frequent misunderstanding of her art as being sociological."[39] The emphasis is therefore less on social history and more about the new possibilities for the image when combined with others, although documentation céline duval does maintain a link to the participants whose photographs she uses. All images are treated equally; they are edited and resized to fit the format of the revue. Here the source of the various images is not identified. Pierre Leguillon writes, "If the family photograph is treated here with the same consideration as an image in a press agency, it is with the purpose of returning full meaning to the subject."[40]

Texts have accompanied boxed sets of

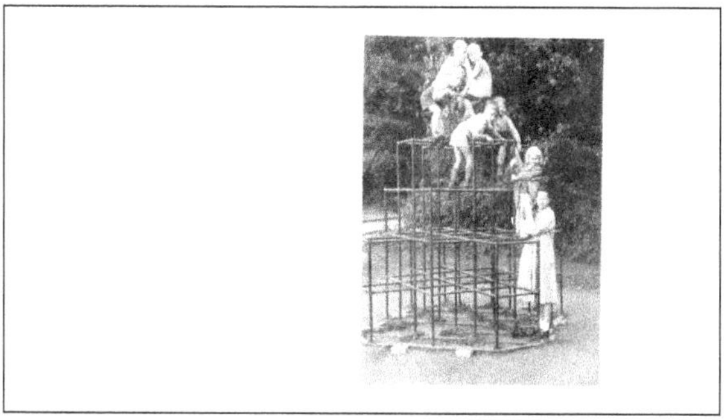

documentation céline duval, revue en 4 images, *édition doc-cd, Houlgate, n°41: construction, co-édition Arko, Nevers, 09/2007. Courtesy of the artist.*

the revue, and the language used is familiar, referencing speech and narrative. "An amateur" writes of the new photos of documentation céline duval as being "mute" [41] and describes her project as "writing a soap opera that isn't there." [42]

While documentation céline duval's recycled images primarily appear in publications, they have also appeared in exhibitions. However the artist has said: "The most appropriate place for this type of image is, I believe, the book. Lately, I have started to accept taking part in exhibitions even though I don't enjoy it really, and I decided to show my images in the form of slide-shows because each image only remains visible for a few seconds and then is pushed out by the next. No sacred effect." [43]

All the projects outlined above exist in

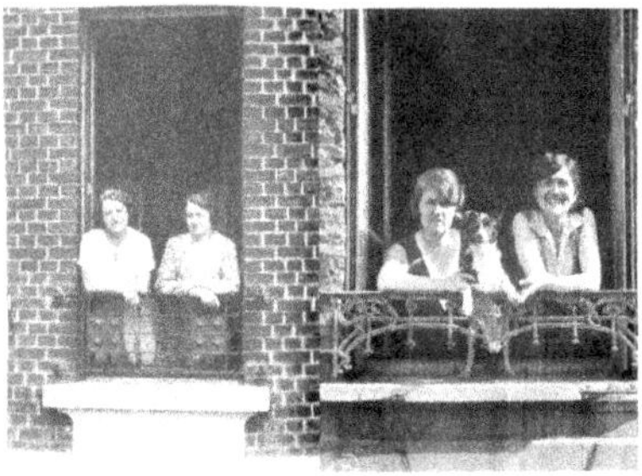

documentation céline duval, revue en 4 images, *édition doc-cd, Houlgate, n°49: portraits, co-édition Artothèque d'Auxerre, 04/2008. Courtesy of the artist.*

both book and exhibition form, just as family photographs may be found in albums and framed on walls and mantelpieces (and stored in boxes and drawers). A bundle of photographs kept in a drawer, or stashed away in a box, can perform the same function as an actual album although with greater informality. The idea of the album can structure the way these groupings are viewed, providing a narrative sequence that is sought after – whether the images are arranged formally, as in an actual album, or informally, as in the case of the bundles of photographs. The album provides a context for the single image, making it possible to compare one instant with another.

The search for meaning in a single snapshot may involve speculation upon other images that might follow or precede it. The construction of memories or narratives based on loose assortments of photographs is a different process to that based on a bound album. The latter is consciously edited and constructed. While it is often intended that it be shown and shared, that access is guarded by its owner, whereas the framed photograph in the home or workplace may be seen by anyone entering the space. The sharing of albums is in a sense performed and accompanied by spoken dialogue. It is something that takes time, which is also required for making an album – for reflection, editing and assembling. This is implicit in all the projects discussed, as the artists recover images otherwise lost, giving them a new life.

NOTES

1 See for example Richard Chalfen, 'Redundant Imagery: Some Observations on the Use of Snapshots in American Culture,' *Journal of American Studies* vol. 4, no. 1 (1981): 106-113.

2 Philip Stokes, 'The Family Photograph Album: So Great a Cloud of Witnesses,' in Graham Clarke (editor), *The Portrait in Photography* (London: Reaktion Books, 1992), 193-205.

3 Dave Kenyon, *Inside Amateur Photography* (London: B.T. Batsford, 1992), 25 – 43.

4 Ibid., 57.

5 Published by Kunstmuseum, Lucerne, 1972.

6 Lynn Gumpert, *Christian Boltanski* (Paris: Flammarion, 1994), 34.

7 Christian Boltanski quoted in Gumpert, *Christian Boltanski*, translated by Francis Cowper, 23.

8 Patricia Holland, 'Introduction: History, Memory and the Family Album,' in *Family Snaps*, eds. Jo Spence and Patricia Holland (London: Virago, 1991), 9.

9 Annette Kuhn, *Family Secrets: acts of memory and imagination*, (London and New York: Verso, 1995) 2.

10 Anne Higonnet, *Pictures of Innocence: The History and Crisis of Ideal Childhood* (London: Thames and Hudson, 1998) 90.

11 Simon Watney, 'Ordinary Boys,' in *Family Snaps*, 29.

12 Published by Steidl, Gottingen, in 2001.

13 Mark Godfrey, 'Photography Found and Lost: On Tacita Dean's Floh,' *October*, Vol. 114 (2005), 95n.

14 Ibid.

15 Ibid., 114.

16 Tacita Dean, 'Analogue,' in *Tacita Dean*, eds. Christina Kennedy and Georgina Jackson (Dublin: Dublin City Gallery The Hugh Lane, 2007), 42.

17 Michael Newman, 'Salvage' *Tacita Dean: Seven Books* (Gottingen: Steidl/ARC/Musée d'Art Moderne de la Ville de Paris, 2003), 'The Collection.'

18 Chalfen, 'Redundant Imagery: Some Observations on the Use of Snapshots' in *American Culture*, 113n.

19 Tacita Dean, 'FLOH,' *Tacita Dean: Seven Books* (Gottingen: Steidl/ARC/Musée d'Art Moderne de la Ville de Paris, 2003)

20 Ibid.

21 Newman, 'Salvage,' 'The Collection.'

22 Mark Godfrey, Photography Found and Lost: On Tacita Dean's Floh," *October*, Vol. 114 (2005): 112.

23 Tacita Dean: *FLOH*, Frith Street Gallery, London, 2 – 29 March 2001.

24 Published by Autograph ABP, London.

25 Mohini Chandra quoted in Cornerhouse Publications' new title information sheet.

26 'Open House: A Conversation about Vox Populi Norway 2004 between Dag Erik Elgin and Fiona Tan,' *Mirror Maker* (Heidelberg: Kehrer Verlag, 2006), 73.

27 Ibid., 77.

28 Published by Bookworks, London, in 2006.

29 Rachel Kent, "Mappo mundi," in Fiona Tan, *VOX POPULI*: Sydney (London: Bookworks, 2006), 124.

30 Ibid., 122.

31 'Open House,' 75.

32 Rachel Kent, "Mappo mundi," in Fiona Tan, *VOX POPULI*: Sydney (London: Bookworks, 2006), 123.

33 Ibid.

34 'Open House,' 81.

35 Suzanne Cotter, "Each and everyone," in Fiona Tan, *VOX POPULI*: Norway (London: Bookworks, 2006), 123.

36 Ibid.

37 Laura McLean-Ferris, "Artist in Residence: documentation céline duval," *www.artreview.com*, 8 December 2008 (http://www.artreview.com/profiles/blogs/artist-in-residence; accessed 26 February 2012)

38 Ibid.

39 François Coadou, documentation céline duval, *reproduction* 2, 2009, 2.

40 Pierre Leguillon, *Conceptual art for families*, 04/2008.

41 An amateur, translated by Ian Walthew, "Our cousins, our parents, our friends," 2006

42 Ibid.

43 Laura McLean-Ferris, "Artist in Residence: documentation céline duval," *www.artreview.com*, 8 December 2008, (http://www.artreview.com/profiles/blogs/artist-in-residence; accessed 26 February 2012)

44 Published by IANNBOOKS, Seoul, 2011.

PRACTICE

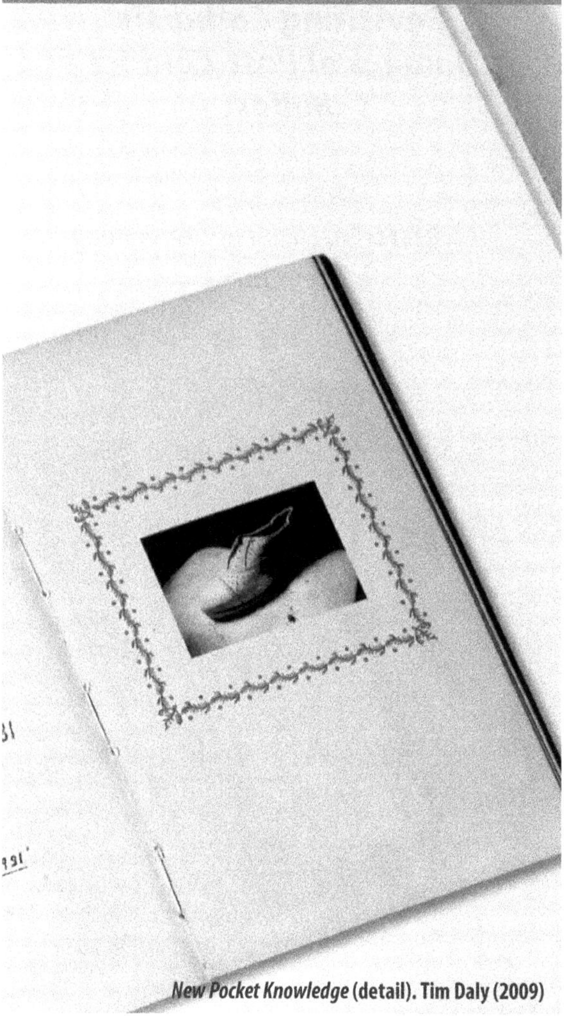

New Pocket Knowledge (detail). Tim Daly (2009)

Book, Exhibition, Lecture, Website – Revisiting *Catharsis: Images of Post-Conflict Belfast*

ANGELA KELLY

Rochester Institute of Technology
New York

The process of making work – from developing a concept, to re-imagining it in process, to distilling the best of it through editing – often leads to a re-thinking of its final material form. If the process leads to a successful resolution, then a new work of art is brought to fruition, though not necessarily to completion. The photographer in the digital age no longer needs to work towards a singular material form or end point. Work may gain new traction long after it was first conceived or developed. Each new context can suggest a new audience or lead to a new interpretation of the work or of photography itself. Artists may distribute work via the internet, create it in digital form for the screen only, develop it as an artist's book, display fine prints in a conventional gallery setting, or any combination of the above.

The body of work, *Catharsis: Images of Post-Conflict Belfast*, an ongoing series of photographs made in Belfast from 2008, is currently disseminated in two forms. First, a conventional portfolio of large-scale prints made for exhibition; and second, a lecture format, one that is partly a live performance and partly visual/textual narrative in the form of a lecture. (A forthcoming website, AngelaKellyPhoto.com introduces the work, *Catharsis* in the context of the genre New Documentary photography.) The question arises, how might the work live beyond the lecture or a particular exhibition space, or exist beyond the artist's personal website? At this juncture, each site of encounter with the work is quite specific. In conceiving a site for the work – whether imagined as large-scale prints in a gallery installation, a website, or in an artist's book – each site potentially holds a memory of its sister site. As such it holds the potential for a dialogue between each of them, suggesting multiple interpretations of it. The nature of each of these different viewing sites will affect how the viewer receives and experiences the work.

To date this work has been primarily shown in gallery settings in the USA and China[1], and disseminated through series of public lectures in the USA and Europe.[2] The idea of re-creating *Catharsis* as an artist's book is a more recent development, one that is still in process and offers yet another way to think about the work itself in terms of both audience and dissemination beyond the gallery and the website. The book format also offers the opportunity to rethink the scale of the work, to explore the role which

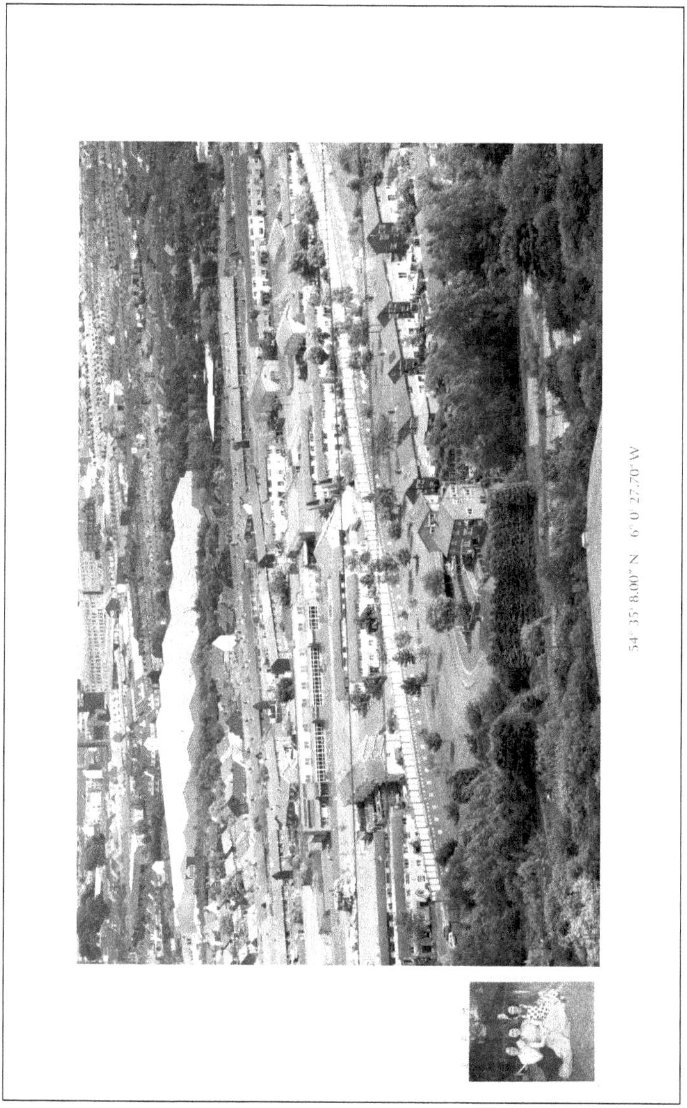

Angela Kelly, Bird's Eye View Belfast with album image of the Somerville Sisters, 2011. *Archival digital photograph. 24x32 inches.*

narrative or text plays in relation to the visual and to consider how the final production values contribute to the overall meaning of the work.

The work in *Catharsis* essentially resembles a series of single pages and in the gallery context becomes a book on the wall. This is a deliberate reference to the conventional family album. The initial public dissemination of the work was made through a panel presentation at the College Arts Association conference in Chicago in 2010. I discussed the work in the context of the panel: *After the Fact: Making a Photographic Record of the Past.*[3] As the work evolved and the opportunity to share it through subsequent lectures developed, the lecture took on a new direction. Rather than simply deliver a formal lecture/report on the work as I did initially at CAA, I later sought to create a live action experience for the audience akin to a participatory performance. The lecture form is neither fixed nor finite, but is itself a potentially creative form, one in which the audience has a role in reshaping through questions and discussion points.

> Catharsis: Images of Post Conflict Belfast *exploits the idea that the meaning of a photograph*

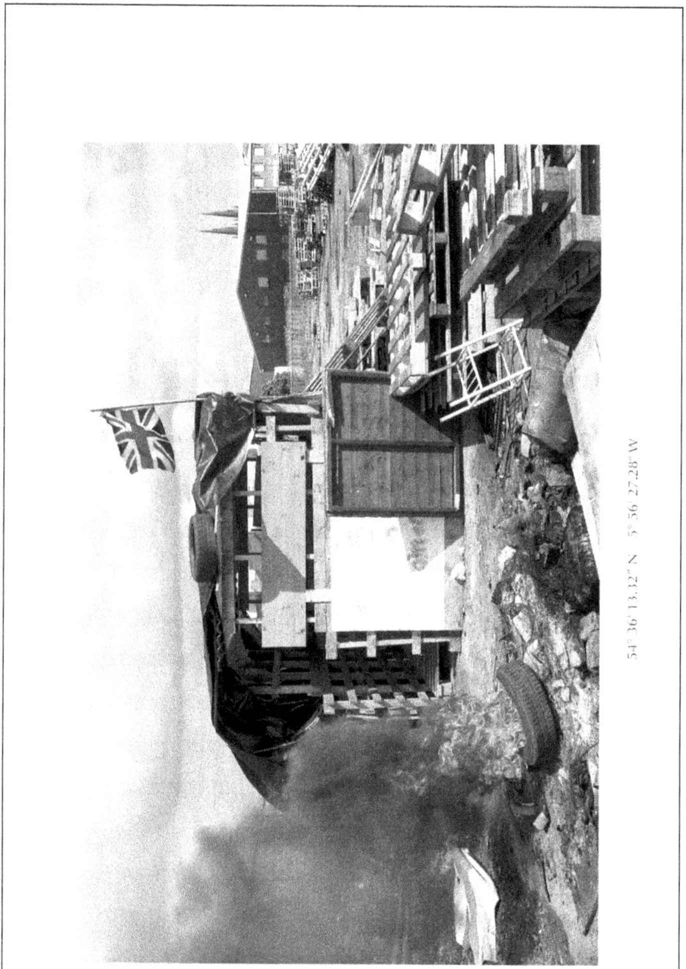

Angela Kelly, Sectarian Bonfire Site, Belfast with album image of Tony and Angela, *2011. Archival digital photograph. 24x32 inches. Collection: the Artist.*

is negotiable. In particular, I am interested in how the photograph is as much a trace of memory as of reality. Photographs resonate with me as repositories of history and can beckon the viewer to a new understanding of place. The concept of loss, memory and history has permeated my photographic work and my teaching of photography for over two decades. Initially personal loss and tragedy provoked a shift in my practice from a socially engaged critical meta-documentary work addressing female identity, issues of homeland and homelessness and the contemporary family. No less critical than former projects, my work shifted to examine the nature of the vernacular image itself within the context of personal and social history. This binding of the social, historical and the personal within a studio arts practice has played out in subtly different, yet complementary, ways in a number of projects. This shift occurred as photography itself shifted gradually from an analog to a digital practice, providing me with an incentive to explore the idea of memory loss and history in a physically layered way. More recently, I have pried the layers apart to explore juxtaposition, rather than layering, a strategy I have returned to but with an entirely different purpose.

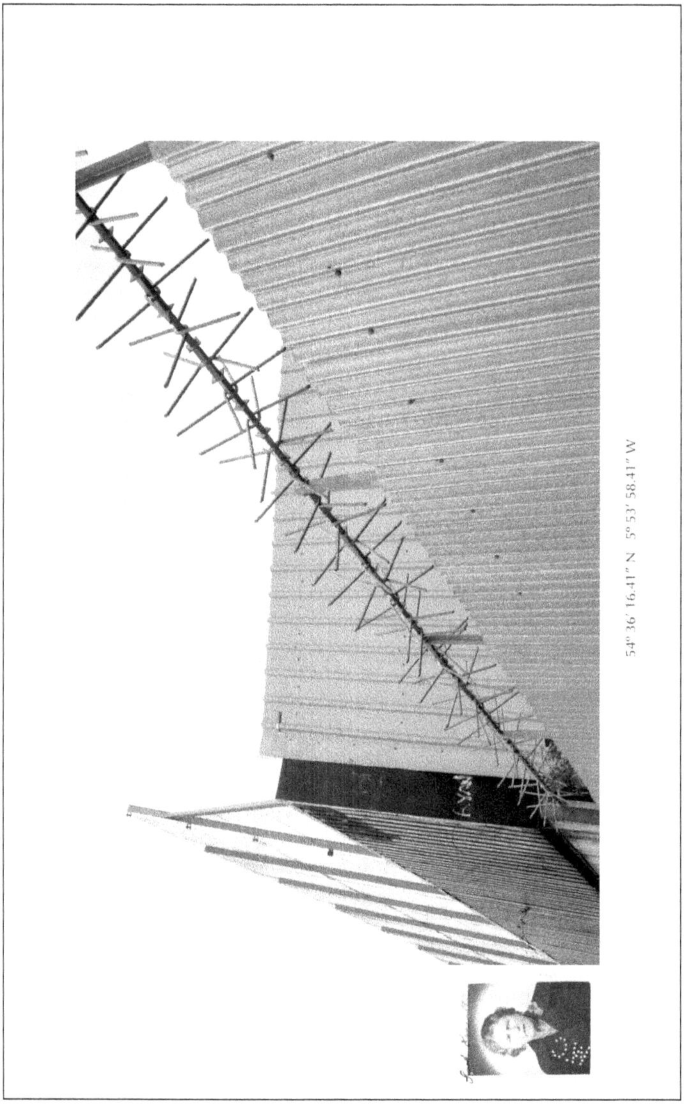

Angela Kelly, Ryan's Tag, Peace Wall, Belfast with album image of Grandmother Sarah, 2011/. *Archival digital photograph. 24x32 inches. Collection: the Artist.*

> *I have been photographing the urban and rural landscape to connect to their particular histories. Photographs made recently in Ireland speak to a post-conflict new Belfast landscape that resonates with my memories of growing up there. In this work, I focus on photographing sites of post-conflict in the loyalist community that have transformed into tourist sites. (Previously, I photographed famine sites in Ireland, which remain invisible to the eye and are virtually unknown.) I often use images in juxtaposition. Family photographs are often appropriated and layered with maps, while landscapes are sometimes embedded with text.*

My proposal for the panel, *After the Fact: Making a Photographic Record of the Past*, was to present one or more of my photo-based projects connected to the idea of loss, memory and history as in the works, *Catharsis* and *Aftermath*. Each project employs different strategies, such as installation, collage, the vernacular photograph or text in combination. *Catharsis* is about the act of remembering. *Aftermath* (Post-Katrina New Orleans) is about the consequences of forgetting.

In *Catharsis*, I revisit the notion of a family

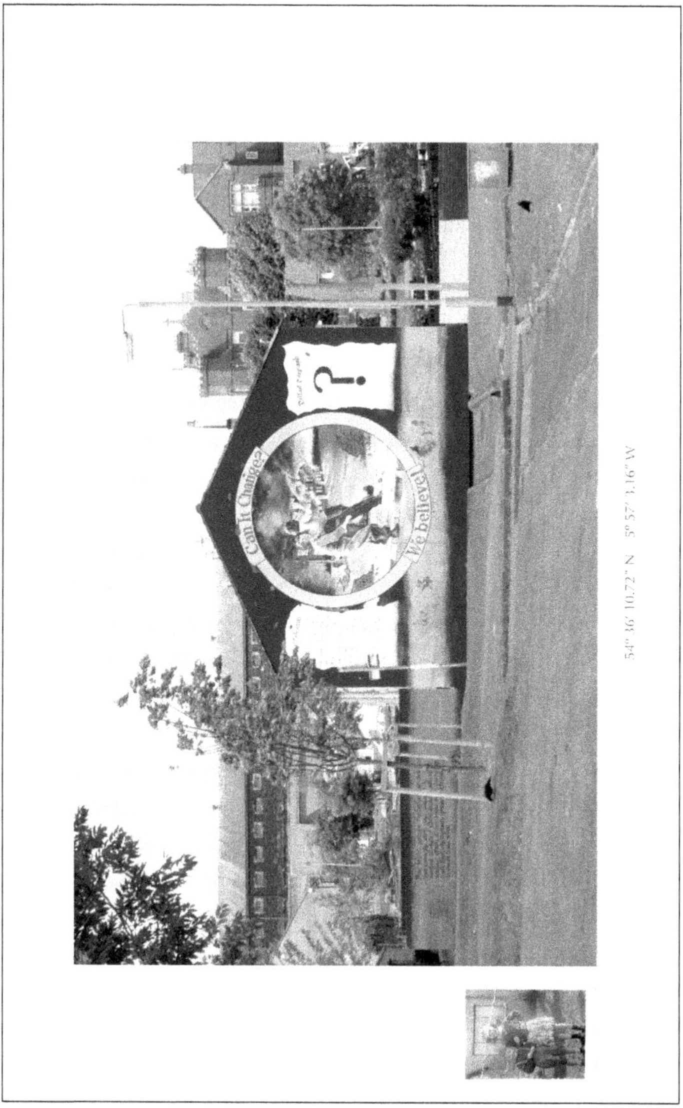

Angela Kelly, Sectarian Mural, Belfast with album image of Angela and Tony, 2011. *Archival digital photograph. 24x32 inches. Collection: the Artist.*

album photograph as a repository of memory. I use vernacular snapshot photographs from my personal family album coupled with new conceptually-driven documentary images that evoke aspects of a city with a war-torn legacy. Each image is marked with its map coordinates as a reference to geographic methods of defining place. It is through the combination of the snapshots, the documentary photographs and the mapping coordinates that the viewer might get a glimpse of how photographic language shapes the myth of our sense of belonging to a place. I developed and refined an artist's statement to accompany *Catharsis* so that viewers would have a starting point or entry into it:

> Artist's Statement
> *Belfast, N. Ireland has a painful history. More recently, I barely recognize the place. It is not so much the idea that Belfast has re-invented itself as part of a new Europe that intrigues me, rather it is the residue or trace of what it once was and still is, coupled with a sense of the new, that I find evocative. I am exploring to what degree the language of the snapshot contributes to, or obscures, our understanding of time and place, since the idea*

> *of knowing someone through their personal images is open to question. The stark contrast in scale and genre, between the personal snapshots and the conceptually driven documentary images, helps shape an understanding of the gap between the personal and the conceptual, mapping out ritual, marking territory and retracing history. While the family album references a site of personal and social identity, the documentary genre can only point to (but never reveal) the subtle and often absent history embedded within it. By engaging the viewer in a dialogue between the familial, the documentary and the geographic, I am creating a space where new questions may be posed.*[4]

Catharsis combines two concepts explored in the previous work *Sundays at Sea*[5] in which I treat the photograph itself as a map by combining it with vernacular family album images and mapping elements from actual physical maps. In *Catharsis*, I make a conceptual leap to tie elements from the separate photographic genres of documentary, art photography and vernacular imagery, inferring new connections between them and reducing the mapping element to GPS coordinates only. Within the structure of the frame, between the intimate album images and the documentary fine art images, I create a conceptual space for catharsis to exist by linking different photographic genres.

Several dualities exist in the work – from the suggestion of formal relationships between unrelated subject matter, to the mirroring of subjects across time, to the shift in scale between the album snapshots and the urban landscapes. These dualities mirror photography's uneasy relationship to the real. Photography is not simply a depiction of reality, nor quite a conveyer of truth or even an outright lie. Photography creates a promise of verisimilitude, acting as a faithful objective witness to a reality which it can't fully deliver. This is one of the reasons I find it so intriguing. Within *Catharsis* I offer a critique of the rhetorical function of photography while, at the same time, I employ it to suggest a tenuous link between memory, history and identity.

To present the work as an artist's book is a new challenge. A book has flow, continuity and an internal logic within its sequence. As an object, the book may function as an exhibition catalog but it also has the potential to be a discrete work of art in itself. It can provide for a richer viewing experience, allowing for the inclusion of additional texts and imagery not included in the exhibit. Through the formal means of a lecture the work is presented in a sequence, in almost filmic narrative terms. The series opens with a bird's eye view of Belfast taken from upon high from the Divis Mountain showing a peace wall[6] that cuts through the landscape below. As the sequence unfolds I move in closer to focus on details of the same wall as seen from above. The viewer soon realises it is the same wall but from a different perspective. Recurring motifs echo throughout the work in subtly different ways. Images of peace walls, razor wire, urban boundaries and fences, loyalist murals and scenes of the docks – all related to post-conflict tourist sites – are both the subject of the work and address the point of view of the photographer. Each image on the gallery wall combines a family album photograph from the past in juxtaposition with an urban landscape from the present. The images are not taken in the same location. The family album photographs reference the site of the album itself. With a few exceptions, the album's images were made in catholic West Belfast, while the contemporary urban documentary images depict the other side of the peace wall within the loyalist protestant community. A dialogue is set up between the two images within the same frame: between the album image and the documentary one; between a father's album snapshots and his daughter's documentary impulse; and between two communities from two distinct eras. These dualities are sometimes playful and political and at other times psychological. Viewing distance is fore-grounded. Due to the shift in scale between the family album images (which are small and intimate) and the urban landscapes (which provide an aura of objectivity) the viewer is invited to move in for an intimate read of the vernacular family image and at the same time to pull back to see the whole, thus pushing and pulling the boundaries of viewing distance. The stance of the photographer and of the viewer becomes a part of the work. He/she is invited to stand in for the photographer using the GPS notation as a place with a militaristic history. Further notions of the relationship between private versus public space are raised. The album photographs are brought into the public sphere and carry with them a trace of the intimate, private album, and while tinged with a sense of 'objectivity' mimic the scientific or technical image associated with the 'real'.

To return to the book form, one strategy for

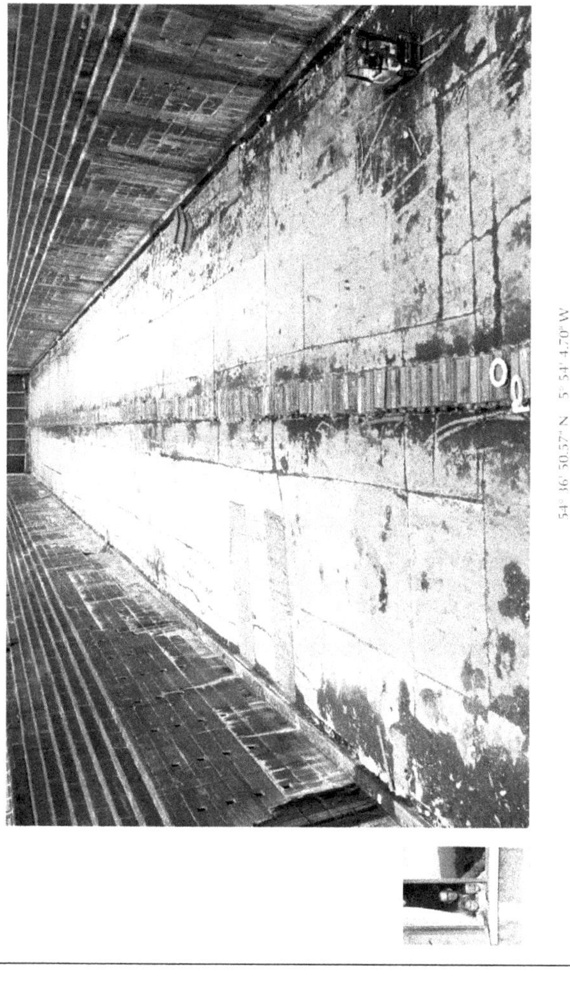

Angela Kelly, Thompson Graving Dock, built for the Titanic, Belfast, with album images of Grandfather William, Angela and Tony, 2011. *Archival digital photograph. 24x32 inches. Collection: the Artist.*

presentation is to show the work as it is presented in the lecture/performance rather than in the gallery presentation form. The work on the gallery wall stresses the physical scale and craft of the work. When presented in the lecture, the work is sequenced to include a close-up of the family photograph while the narrative voice moves the work along. Within the context of a book, the viewer can experience how the images are designed to be read in relationship to each other and then pause on the details of the smaller album image repeated and enlarged within the book format. Again, this echoes the lecture form where I follow each combination image with a close-up view of its related album photograph. As the images shift from the private family album to the gallery, to the website or to the artist's book, each new context provides an opportunity to rethink the importance of the private photograph in our lives. In turn, each re-staging of the documentary photographs in concert with album images point to a reworking of the convention of the documentary genre itself, opening up a space for further interpretation of the 'reality' effect of photography. This slippage between the sites of dissemination blurs the boundaries between them yet reveals their differences. Within all four sites – the lecture, the gallery, the website and the book – the artist offers a way for the audience to enter into a dialogue with the work to engage them in a multiplicity of ways around the use and meaning of photography.

NOTES

1 Exhibitions

Catharsis: Images of Post-Conflict Belfast in "Regarding Place: Photo Media Invitational" 2012, Tower Fine Art Gallery, at the College of Brockport, State University of New York featuring work that uses photography.

Catharsis: Images of Post-Conflict Belfast, 3rd International Photography Exhibition, The Dali Museum, Dali, Yunnan Province. China, September 2011.

2 Lectures

Angela Kelly, "Catharsis: Images of Post-Conflict Belfast," 1st International Photo Media Conference, Aalto University, Helsinki, Finland, April 2012.

Angela Kelly, "Catharsis: Images of Post-Conflict Belfast," Family Ties Conference, University of London, March 2012.

Angela Kelly, "Catharsis: Images of Post-Conflict Belfast," The College at Brockport, SUNY, January, 2012.

Angela Kelly, "Catharsis: Images of Post-Conflict Belfast,'" University of Salford, October 2011.

Angela Kelly, "Catharsis: Images of Post-Conflict Belfast," University of Plymouth, October 2011.

Angela Kelly, "Catharsis: Images of Post-Conflict Belfast," University of Cumbria, November, 2011.

Angela Kelly, "Catharsis: Images of Post-Conflict Belfast," College Arts Association, Chicago, February 2010.

3 Artist's statement

Eventually, a segment of the CAA presentation formed the basis of my artist statement for *Catharsis: Images of Post Conflict Belfast*.

4 Website

http:// www.AngelaKellyPhoto.com. *Sundays at Sea*

(Exhibited at the Hartnett Gallery, Rochester, NY, 1999.)

5 CAA Formal Paper Proposal

Catharsis: Images of Post Conflict Belfast, Panel Presentation:

After the Fact: Making a Photographic Record of the Past.

College Arts Association National Conference, Chicago, February 2010.

6 A peace wall or line is a barrier wall that separates catholic and protestant working class neighbourhoods in Belfast.

Space – Time – Fragment: Conceptual Documentary Photography in the Artist's Book as a Tool of Analysis

ELISABETH NEUDÖRFL
Folkwang University
Essen, Germany

Often, the sequencing in photographic artists' books is used to relate images that were taken at different places and at different times to each other. These images might share similar subject matter and form a narrative; they might also show differing or even opposing subject matter in order to add meaning to one another (e.g. Walker Evans, *American Photographs*; Robert Frank, *The Americans*)[1]. Alternatively, the sequencing can combine several photographs of the same place taken within a very short period of time (e.g. Ed Ruscha, *Every Building on the Sunset Strip*)[2]. This chapter will explore the consequential photographic analysis of space and time using the example of my artist's book *E.D.S.A.*[3]

E.D.S.A. shows photographs taken along Epifanio Delos Santos Avenue (E.D.S.A.) in Metro Manila in the Philippines. Its 26 chapters show between two and seven single photographs taken from the same spot, within seconds, in a panning mode. I will discuss the opportunities the rearrangement of the photographs on double pages creates for the viewer to gain knowledge about this specific space (E.D.S.A from a pedestrian's viewpoint) and its specific course of time. This photobook emphasises the fragmentary character of photography, using the fragments to build a coherent narrative without straightening out the fragmentation. In this way it deals with aspects of space, assuming that space is not given but constituted by the movement of people.[4]

On the street, at these specific spots, looking at E.D.S.A. and its cross streets and surroundings makes apparent the possibility of several spaces at the same site. I suggest that, as a journey along E.D.S.A. is inevitable in Manila, the examination of space in connection with time becomes a social investigation about the different social groups using different spaces on it.

As a point of reference, and to differentiate between diverse methods of sequencing photographs in a book, I want to describe some photographs from Robert Frank's *The Americans*, a book that has taught me and countless other photographers valuable lessons in this respect.

It is not possible to define a beginning or an end of the sequence, as the whole book is a single sequence with many overlapping narratives. Any selection of several succeeding photographs would be merely random. Here I discuss the photographs in the exact order in which they appear in the book.

The layout of the book is very simple. *The*

Americans contains 83 photographs, always showing one photograph in the middle of a right page, the left page displaying the caption.[5]

The extract I have chosen starts with #32, *U.S. 91–Leaving Blackfoot, Idaho.* It shows two young men in the front of a car, the photographer obviously on board. The car goes from left to right; the photographer, being a passenger, is sitting on the right-hand side. These circumstances leave the car travelling in our usual reading direction. Thinking of the double page spread which leaves the blank page to the left of the photograph, the car moves out of the book, not into it. In the next photograph, #33, *St. Petersburg, Florida*, a car is passing in the background, going in the same direction, i.e. from left to right. In the foreground there are two benches back to back, the upper surface of the backrest vertical in the lower centre of the image. Several senior citizens are sitting there, those on the left looking left, those on the right looking right. The seniors are static; the car is moving, blurred by its motion.

In the next photograph, #34, *Covered Car–Long Beach, California*, we see an urban environment. In front of a single-storey building, depicted frontally, the road kerb parallel to the bottom line of the photograph, a car under a tarpaulin reflects the light so the car is the brightest object in the photograph. It looks very shiny, and although we cannot see the car itself but only its shape beneath the tarpaulin, the car appears glorified. Then, the scenery changes completely. Instead of sun and palm trees, #35, *Car Accident–U.S. 66 between Winslow and Flagstaff, Arizona* shows us bad weather, a rural setting with grassland in the foreground and some buildings in the background. Four people are standing behind a dead person, obviously a traffic victim, covered with a blanket. The shape of the blanket reminds us of the shape of the covered car, but this time there is nothing shiny at all. The blanket is dark and blends in with the surroundings. By means of the similar shapes, Frank very strongly connects these two different photographs, taken at different sites.

Although the photograph with the dead body might seem like a closing picture, the sequence goes on. In the next photograph, #36, *U.S. 285–New Mexico*, we see a highway reflecting the sun. The asphalt seems to glow, making the road appear very promising, comparable to the shiny cover over the car in front of the palm trees. We see a bright strip, stretching in a straight line towards the horizon.

This glowing we see again in the American flag in the next photograph, #37, *Bar–Detroit*. The flag is framed by pictures of Washington and Lincoln, the camera tilted upwards. Thus, Frank connects the wide landscape and its acquisition explicitly with the idea of America.

Throughout the entire book, *The Americans*, the connections between the photographs rely on aspects of form and content across many levels. The formal connections result from similar shapes and lines and go as far as abstract similarities or oppositions in light and shadow. With regard to content, some themes appear again and again, others form sub-sequences. There are photographs succeeding one another within one theme or showing contrasting themes or contrasting aspects of the same theme.

In *Every Building on the Sunset Strip*, Ed Ruscha applies a completely different approach to sequencing. Ruscha photographed the entire Sunset Strip in Los Angeles. He had a camera installed on his car, drove along the street and took pictures at such a rate that every building was depicted. He did that in both directions, showing both sides of the street. *Every Building on the Sunset Strip* is a concertina fold. Ruscha mounted the photographs together so that there is one very long image for each side of the street. Thus, Ruscha outwits the fragmentary character of book pages, constructing one long image with some cars and people turning up repeatedly. The concertina fold is more than eight metres long.

For my book *E.D.S.A.*, the starting point was a street (as in *Every Building on the Sunset Strip*), but I did not wish to depict it in its entirety (and it has that in common with *The Americans*, which did not aim at encyclopaedically depicting the United States of America). Within the sequences that were taken from a single vantage point, the individual photographs are strongly connected. This connection was already intended at the time they were taken. The selection of the sequences, the length of the sequences and the order of the sequences (i.e. their sequencing) in the book are the result of editorial decisions.

E.D.S.A. consists of 288 pages showing 232 images of 116 different photographs. This means that every photograph is shown twice, first on a right page and then on the subsequent left page. The photographs are arranged in 26 chapters, and I will refer to each chapter as a sequence. The sequences are separated from each other by two blank pages, physically one blank sheet of paper. Each sequence is characterised by the fact that it has been photographed from one defined vantage point within a very short span of time. All the images are the same size, with a white margin on all four sides. Other than the title and the publishing information, the book has no text, not even page numbers. On the cover, there is a stylised map of E.D.S.A. showing how it runs in a wide curve through the different cities of Metro Manila.[6]

E.D.S.A. is an unavoidable thoroughfare, which leads to the fact that it is used by all social groups. It is also one of the most important public spaces in Manila. In 1986, it served as the site of demonstrations for the People Power Revolution against the regime of President Ferdinand Marcos, which is also known as the E.D.S.A. Revolution. That revolution was successful and led to the ousting of Marcos. In 2001, protesters again used E.D.S.A. for the peaceful overthrow of President Joseph Estrada. The demonstrations against Estrada are called the E.D.S.A. Revolution of 2001 or E.D.S.A. II. Four months later, supporters of Estrada gathered on E.D.S.A.; this failed attempt to reinstate Estrada as president is called E.D.S.A. III. Although

E.D.S.A. as a street serves literally everybody regardless of social status, E.D.S.A. Revolution and E.D.S.A. II are perceived as movements of the middle and upper classes in contrast to E.D.S.A. III which was an uprising of the lower classes who were in support of President Estrada. Thus, even in such an accessible place as a public street, the masses who express their political will are separated by social status. It is worth noting that the people could not accomplish their objective.

None of this history is, of course, perceptible when walking along the street.[7] But the street, as most streets, has the potential to be a place for political expression. Its accessibility is visible. I am particularly interested in the street as a social space, a place not only for vehicular travel, but also as a space where social actualities, involving all economic groups, take place and can be observed. What we see tells us about something abstract like the patterns of society. The different social groups do not mingle on E.D.S.A. One obvious social characteristic is speed – depending on their social status, people use cars, trains, buses, jeepneys, motorbikes, bicycles, or they walk. Those who can afford it sit in the back of their cars, behind their driver, protected by tinted windows, air-conditioned, in a space totally isolated from their surroundings. Less well-off traffic participants share their in-vehicle space not only with strangers, but also with heat, dust, noise, pollution and the like.

The main function of the street is transit, but the street is also a workplace for public service staff, who clean, who construct, who control traffic. It is a space for small businesses, to clean windshields, to sell newspapers or household items, to beg. Economic and social reality becomes apparent on the street, but it is perceived differently by the different parties. I suggest that for those using cars, the reality inside the car prevails over the reality on the street.

It is important that the photographs in *E.D.S.A.* show people. These people are depicted in action, which is a first indication that I am dealing with the matter of space here. The individuals that we see (and also those we don't see because they are hidden in their cars) constitute space by moving through the city and by employing the city. This means that there are different spaces on this site, constituted by different people through different actions.

I don't want to argue that *E.D.S.A.* is less *built*

up (or constructed) than *The Americans*, but I think that it leads not so much to the formation of a narrative but to an analysis. Perhaps it forms a narrative about society in Manila, and analyses space and time. Before I constructed my view of E.D.S.A., I had explicitly fragmented it. The sequencing does not repeat the reality from which the fragments were taken; it does not restore a continuity. It is a re-arrangement that includes a shift in relation to reality.

After I had chosen E.D.S.A. as the subject of my photographs, I faced the compositional problem resulting from its very length. When walking along it, one's view always follows its long shape: the lanes of the street and the fronts of the bordering buildings with the respective compositional elements such as lines, diagonals, etc. Although it is a relatively wide street, its width is insignificant compared to its length. Without wanting to take panoramic pictures, I started to think about the panorama as an idea, about *vedutas* as relevant city views of a specific time and about what a relevant city view today might look like.

In his book *Fish Story*[8] Allan Sekula describes his search for a valid representation of the sea in photography, thinking about the classic panorama and the seascape. He links the disappearance of visual representation of "the sea" to the emergence of the – potentially invisible – submarine in the beginning of the 20th century.[9] Sekula also reflects upon globalization and capitalism. As regards different spaces at one site and the separation of people of different social status, he makes similar observations to mine.[10]

Although dealing with the sea and not with the city, Sekula reveals a connection between the sea and the city dating back to the 19th century. He marvels at the visionary strength in Friedrich Engels' writings which is expressed in the quick jump from the panoramic view from a ship on the River Thames onto the notorious city streets within a few pages.[11] Here, Sekula finds a valid depiction:

> *As it moves at the center of its own panorama, the ship becomes the lost and wandering daughter of the land. One measure of Engels' radicality was his ability to break with the fatalism of this emerging romance of the sea's isolation, and to step from the deck of the ship onto the streets of the city at the center of the global circle of power.*[12]

In contrast to the idea behind the classic panorama, I was not looking for an overview in one photograph, and I wanted to avoid implicit hierarchies in my photographs.

When photographing the sequences, every exposure is the logical consequence of the previous one and is not purposefully made or chosen; thus, it is incidental rather than intentional (which is of course not entirely true – I will come back to this). The aspect ratio of the street is not only reflected in the aspect ratio of the panorama, but also the disorganized street life leads to disorganization within the photographs. This last notion may be supported by the fact that the vertical format of the single photograph stands against the idea of 'wideness' in the panorama.

When photographing, I assumed that it was not possible to depict everything that I wanted, standing at one spot, in one picture. Or, better: in one picture that met my own pictorial demands. So I decided to split things up into several pictures. I stood at one spot, started with one fragment, turned, and took the next photograph so it would slightly overlap with the previous one. This means that the framing depends on what lies beyond each photograph's left or right border much more than on the idea of a single balanced picture. Of course the framing was not completely determined by the first photograph I took. I could still move the camera to the right and to the left, and even more so up and down, as I intended that the pictures shifted up and down against each other. As the frame was relatively fixed, time and movement came into place. I did not move, but people and vehicles around me did, shifting against each other from second to second and from one picture to the next. This movement in time results in an experience of space (see Figures 1–7).

Producing *E.D.S.A.* happened in several phases that were clearly separated chronologically. After the research, I photographed; and after I had completed photographing, I started editing or working with the material. I was looking for an adequate way to show the pictures, trying various ways, various sizes, etc. I looked at them for some time, at the single pictures and at mounted sequences, and I decided that it could only work as a book, for several reasons. Mounting several adjacent photographs together as a wide panorama produced an overview and denied the fragmentation that had happened while taking the photographs. This was not an option, since

I felt I had to intensify the fragmentation in order to reconstruct an authentic and slightly disorientating experience for the viewer. Perhaps even more importantly, the aspect of time had to be put into perspective with the time that passes while looking at the photographs. On the one hand, the crucial characteristic of photography employed here is fragmentation. Every photograph shows a spatio-temporal fragment of the world that existed in front of the camera at the time of the exposure.[13] Because photographs show movement at one given moment, bringing the movement to a stop, the viewer gains time to see all the things that are depicted, perhaps better than he or she could see them in reality, when they are in movement. The fragmentation results from the limitation caused by the frame and the limitation at the moment of the exposure. Thus, the course of time is stopped, and the reality on the street becomes evident: people, vehicles, plants, billboards, kiosks and more.

On the other hand, the book constructs a quasi-filmic experience for the viewer as the pages are turned. In the book one can see only two photographs at once. After turning the page, the previous spread is no longer visible; only the new spread is visible. Yet the previous spread lies like a layer in the perception of the viewer under the new spread. While turning the pages, time passes. The viewer chooses the speed of turning the pages. I assume that he or she needs more time than that which passed between taking one picture and the next. Perception is slowed down. Every sequence starts on a right-hand page, and every photograph is shown on a right-hand page first and then repeated on the next left-hand page, in precisely the same physical place, as it were, on one sheet of paper (*recto* and *verso*) separated only by the fibre of the paper. The viewer's advance through the book is only half as fast as it could have been. It is easy to follow the continuity from one photograph to the next on a double page spread. However, if the reader follows from one photograph on a right-hand page to the next photograph on the next left-hand page (bearing in mind the necessity to turn the page), identifying the continuity is difficult. So, the duplication of the photographs also maintains the connections between the adjacent photographs.

While following the movement of the camera through the pictures, and following the movement of people and cars at the same time, all of a sudden, the movement between photographs is reversed (see Figures 8–12). So I not only slow down the movement on the street, I even turn it around. People seem to walk backwards. The construction of the perception of the street in the photographs relates to the construction of our perception of a street in reality. In the sequencing, these constructions are obvious and an issue of the book. Through the construction of the book, through the editing, I demonstrate its own construction, I demonstrate the time passing between pictures, I demonstrate the construction in the process of perception and the construction of the representation of the world in photography.

Figures 1-18
Elisabeth Neudörfl, from: E.D.S.A. *(Berlin: Wiens Verlag, 2010).*
Colour photograph, double page spread. All images © Elisabeth Neudörfl.
Courtesy of Elisabeth Neudörfl/Galerie Barbara Wien Wilma Lukatsch Berlin.

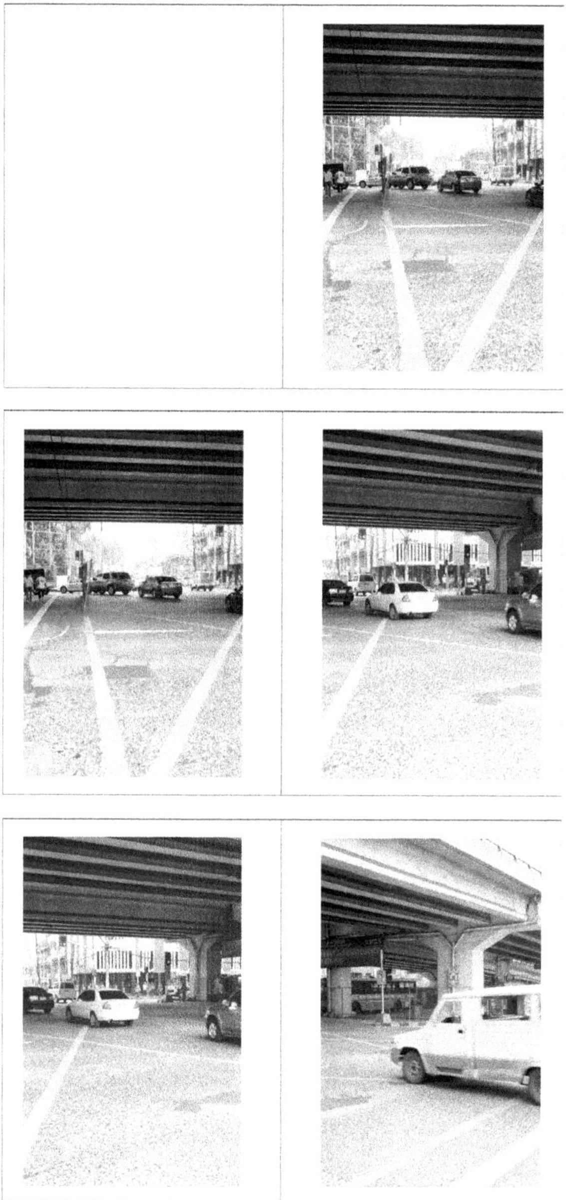

Figures 1-3

Figures 4-6

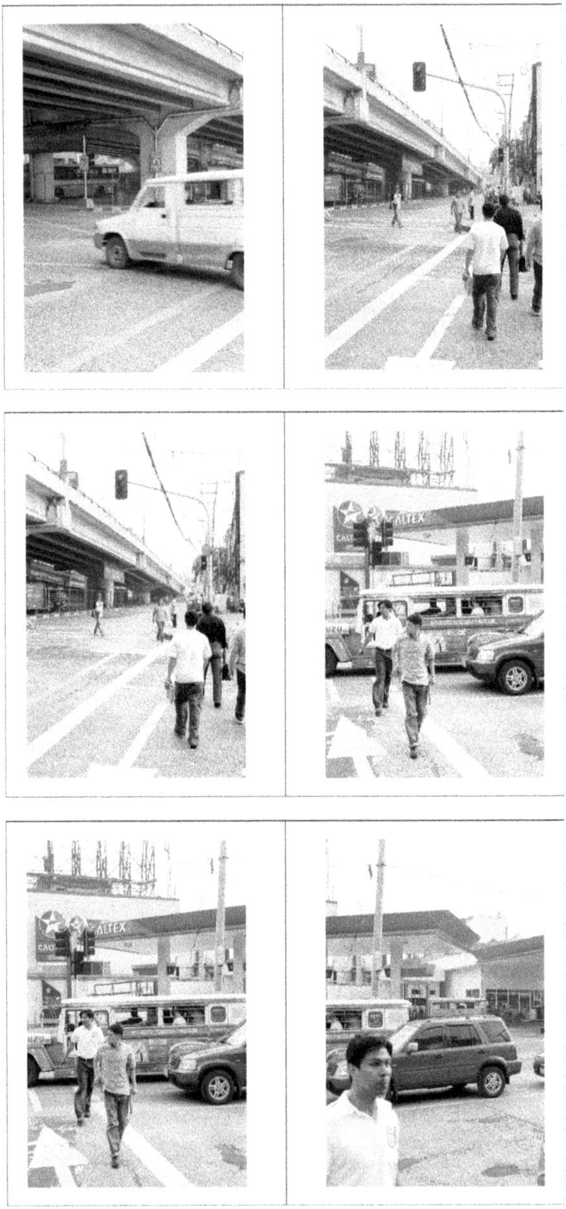

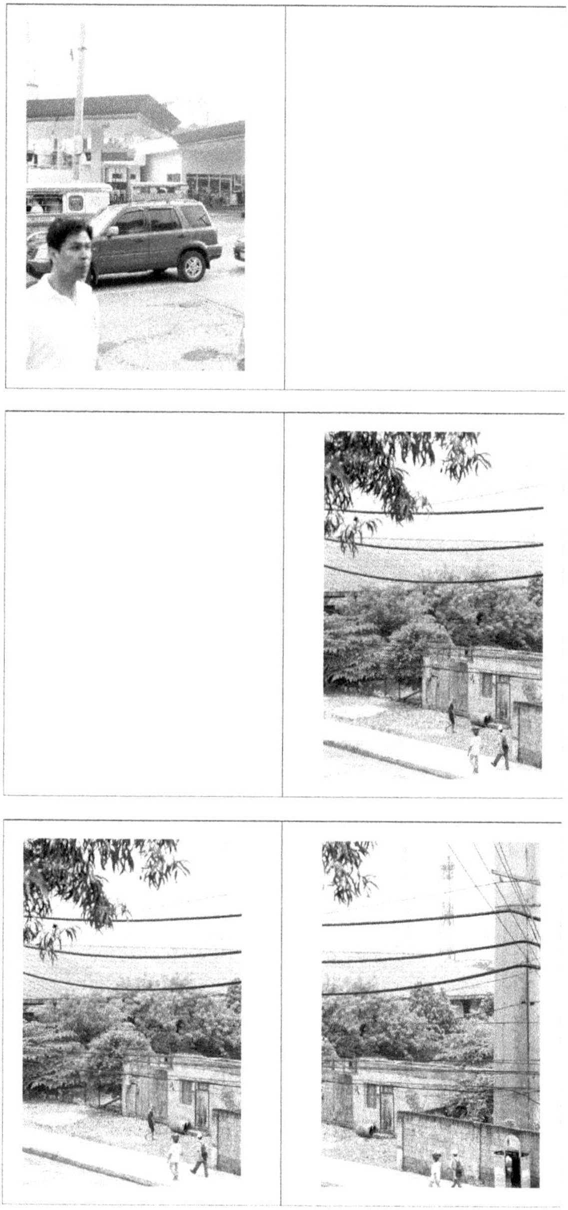

Figures 7-9

Figures 10-12

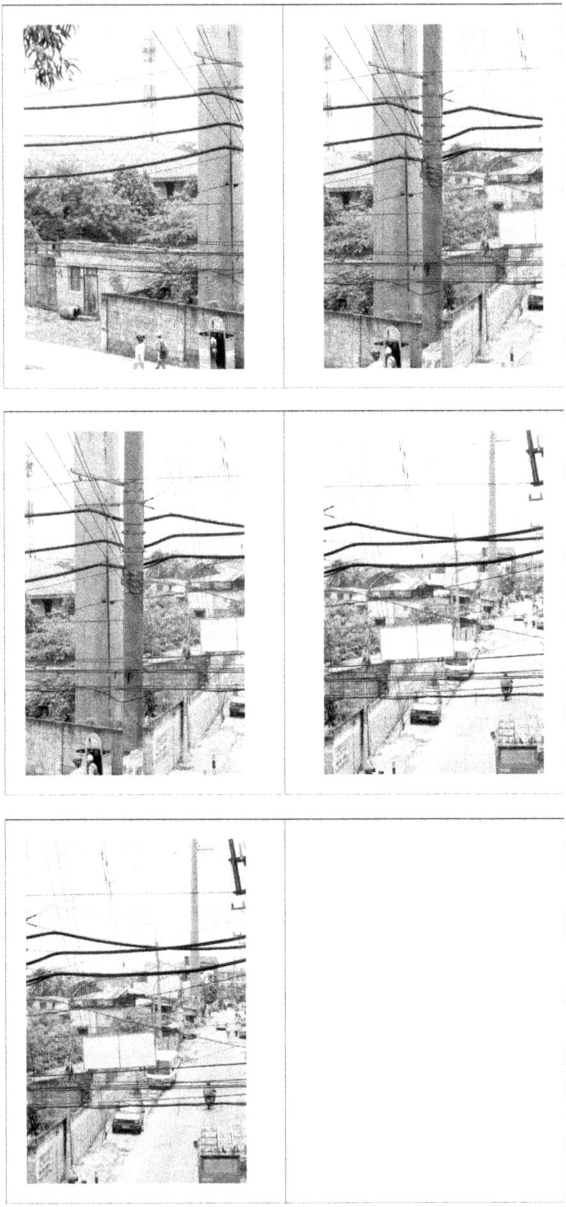

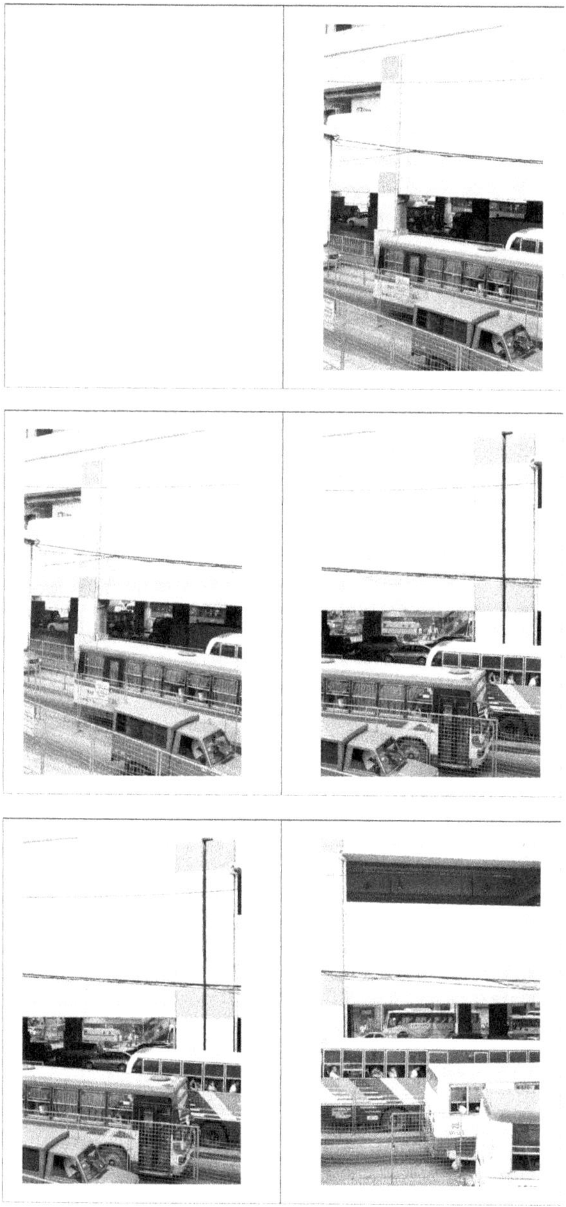

Figures 13-15

Figures 16-18

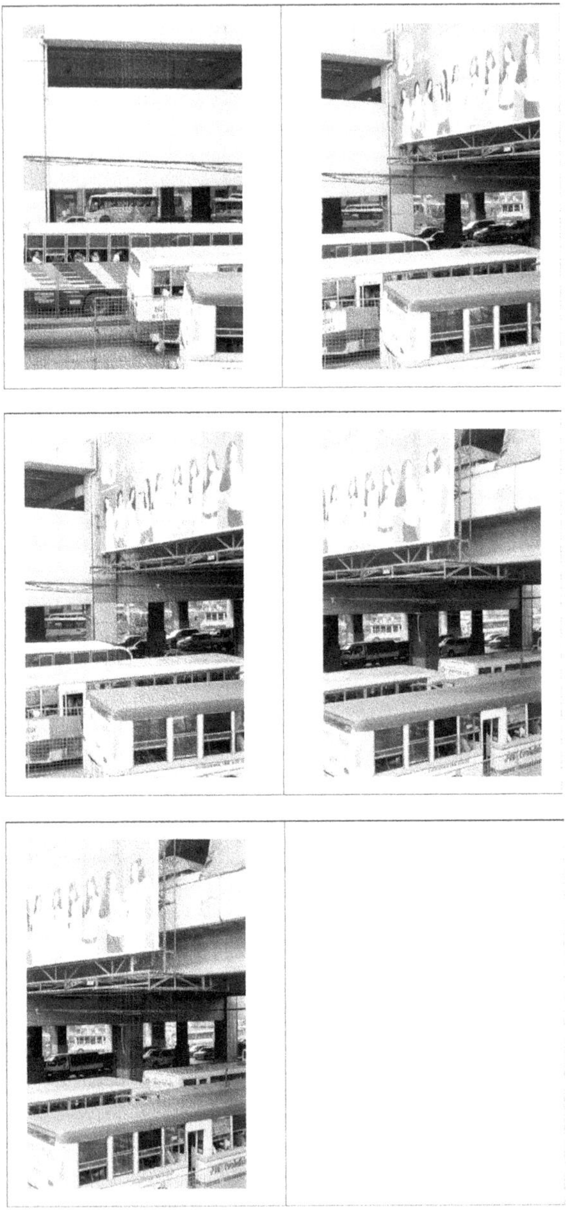

NOTES

1 Walker Evans, *American Photographs* (New York: Museum of Modern Art, 1938). Robert Frank, *The Americans* (New York: Grove Press, 1959).

2 Ed Ruscha, *Every Building on the Sunset Strip* (Los Angeles, 1966).

3 Elisabeth Neudörfl, *E.D.S.A.* (Berlin: Wiens Verlag, 2010).

4 See Martina Löw, *Raumsoziologie* (Frankfurt a.M.: Suhrkamp, 2001).

5 The book was first published as *Les Americains* by Delpire in Paris, France, in 1958. The photographs in the original book were accompanied by texts in French which were placed on the left pages. The first American edition and various other editions came without the texts of the French edition and included an essay by Jack Kerouac at the beginning of the book. The captions were on the left pages, next to the respective photographs. The same also applies to the new edition of 2008, which was overseen by Frank (Göttingen: Steidl, 2008). In various editions in the 50 years in between, some had page numbers on the left page with the captions listed in the back of the book. "The Americans by Robert Frank, Steidl/National Gallery of Art", accessed February 17, 2012, http://www.steidlville.com/books/766-Die-Amerikaner-Deutsche-Ausgabe.html

6 E.D.S.A. runs, from south to north, through the cities of Pasay, Makati, Mandaluyong, San Juan, Quezon City, and Caloocan.

7 On E.D.S.A., at the corner with White Plains Avenue in Quezon City, is the People Power Monument commemorating the People Power Revolution. On the corner with Ortigas Avenue is the E.D.S.A. Shrine, or Shrine of Mary, Queen of Peace, Our Lady of E.D.S.A., built

in 1989. Not far from E.D.S.A., in Makati City at the corner Ayala Avenue with Paseo de Roxas is the Monument to Immortality for Benigno Aquino, Jr., whose assasination provoked the uprising against president Marcos in 1986.

8 Allan Sekula, *Fish Story* (Düsseldorf: Richter, 1995).

9 Ibid., p. 110.

10 Ibid., p. 51.

11 ibid. p. 42.

12 Ibid., p. 48.

13 See Abigail Solomon-Godeau, "Who is Speaking Thus? Some Questions About Documentary Photography", in *Photography at the Dock: Essay on Photographic History, Institutions, and Practices* (Minneapolis: University of Minnesota Press, 1991), 169-83.

PPP: Preston, Paris, Process

ADAM MURRAY
Preston is my Paris &
University of Central Lancashire

DIANE SMYTH
British Journal of Photography

This conversation between Adam Murray and Diane Smyth took place via email between 23rd February 2012 and 28th March 2012. Endnotes have been added subsequently in order to assist further research.

From: Adam Murray
To: Diane Smyth
Date: Thu, Feb 23, 2012 at 3.26pm
Subject: Preston, Paris, Process

Hello Diane
How are you? I've been thinking about this conversation we're going to be having over the next few weeks and to begin with I feel that it is important to give a small amount of context with regards the project that will provide the main focus – *Preston is my Paris.*[1]

I co-founded *Preston is my Paris* in June 2009 with Robert Parkinson whilst we were both living in Preston, Lancashire. Our first publication had very modest intentions and was simply a black and white, photocopied zine that we printed on the office photocopier, hand stapled and folded and distributed an edition of 50 around Preston for free. The contents were a variety of visual items such as our own original photographs, found photographs, letters, scanned objects; the one link being that they were all either taken or found in Preston. Over 18 months we produced 15 issues of this zine and decided to end the series when I relocated to London and Robert moved to Manchester.

Since then, the project has developed into a large body of photographic work that combines original photographic projects, printed publications, live events and digital applications with intentions of investigating themes relating to everyday life and social consciousness.

Our work has been recognised as being an important part of the recent movement of self-publishing that has occurred in photographic culture, however, I am always slightly concerned that because a work is self-published, this aspect takes over as the primary point of interest and the photographic content is almost a secondary concern. So perhaps we can start with that, what are your thoughts about the role the photographs have in the *Preston is my Paris* work and also the self publishing/photobook culture as a whole?
Regards
Adam

From: Diane Smyth
To: Adam Murray
Sent: Sun, Mar 4, 2012 at 6.15pm
Subject: Preston, Paris, Process

Hi Adam

Sorry to take so long to get back to you – I've been being kept busy with the *Art Book Fair*[2] in Cardiff last weekend and the *B Book Show*[3] in London this weekend. It's interesting to see how self-publishing is taking off in the UK, and that an infrastructure such as book fairs and exhibitions is springing up to help photographers and artists share and distribute their work. I think *Preston is my Paris* stands out though, because of the seamless integration between the type of photographs you take, and the way that you distribute them.

Your photographs capture everyday scenes, such as an unremarkable street on an unremarkable housing estate in *Routes 1*[4], or the view from a train in *Thank You For Travelling with Northern Rail*[5]; it seems to me that the low-key way in which you choose to publish and distribute this work expands on its subject matter. Rather than creating an expensive photobook, you create zines with everyday tools such as photocopiers, thereby keeping the books affordable and approachable. By creating physical photobooks, rather than relying on a website or blog, you make it easier to get them in front of people. Is that a deliberate tactic? How closely did you think through the distribution and mode of production of your work before you started?

You've mentioned to me in the past that you were inspired by Georges Perec and his investigation of everyday life, for example, the *Place Saint-Sulpice*[6] in Paris in 1974, in which over three days he attempted to note the comings-and-goings around him. Perec's investigations were part of an attempt to make people more aware of the texture of their lives, to notice small details "so that they may at last speak of what is, of who we are?" as he wrote in *L'Infra-ordinaire.*[7] Do you see PPP [Preston is my Paris Publishing] as being aligned with Perec in that attempt? Is self-publishing part of the strategy?
Thanks
Di

From: Adam Murray
To: Diane Smyth
Sent: Thu, Mar 8, 2012 at 3.35pm
Subject: Preston, Paris, Process

Hello Di
No problem at all, yes there has been a lot of photobook events, fairs and festivals starting in up the UK over the last 2 or 3 years hasn't there. It definitely seems to be an international movement as well, which is interesting. From my own experience though the standard of the events seems to be very mixed; some are genuinely innovative, show exciting independently or small publisher produced work that has clearly been curated by event organisers with a strong sense of identity and purpose for the event. Others unfortunately just seem to be put together because that is the thing to do at the moment and end up being more like arts and craft fairs rather than the artists' or photography book events that they are billed as. Have you found any of the events you have attended particularly interesting? What factors have you found make a good photobook event?

I'm glad that the photographs and production

of the publications appear seamless as this is definitely the intention, particularly once we moved on to producing the individual 'photo story' type projects. With the original *Preston is my Paris* zines, the production decisions were very much dictated by necessity. Robert and I wanted to follow in the great tradition of fanzines and simply produce the publication about a subject we have great passion for, the city of Preston, and get the publications out to a local audience in the most affordable way possible. I was lucky that I had access to a decent photocopier in the office where I work as a lecturer so each issue cost us very little. We then held launch events in local pubs and gave the zine away for free around the city. I definitely think that the decision to make a physical publication rather than just a blog or online digital publication helped to get the work noticed though, as it is very easy to get completely missed in such a saturated visual space that the internet has become.

As the overall project developed into the photo stories, black & white zines and colour newspapers, the mode of production became a much more conscious conceptual decision. It has always been the intention to make photographic publications that are accessible and this takes a number of forms; affordability is crucial as we recognised that a lot of people are not able to justify spending over £30 on a single photobook, but this does not necessarily mean that they do not want to engage with photobooks. Certain modes of production can also be quite intimidating for those audiences outside of a typical 'art crowd' and we wanted to make publications that people felt comfortable looking through without feeling as if they should be wearing white gloves or even that the work is too precious to pick up at all. Consequently we began to appropriate vernacular forms of printed matter, such as photocopying, photographic prints produced by the local chemist and newsprint.

One point of criticism that has occurred with our mode of production is the limited print run of each work – with the black & white zines it is usually 50 copies and the newspapers between 500-1000. A couple of people have discussed this, such as Jason Evans[8], "I'd argue that the limited run of the some of their publications is, perhaps, at odds with their overarching intentions," and Benedict Burbridge[9], "So why number individual copies as part of a limited supply? Through this small act, the photographers artificially rarefy their products, making a virtue of their exclusivity." What do you think about the limited edition concept in relation to our work but also photobooks in general?

Going back to distribution briefly, one point that I think is crucial to make is that although the intention of the majority of photobook makers is still to produce a physical, printed outcome, the role digital technology plays cannot be underestimated. This has undoubtedly been crucial in the production of work with desktop publishing and cheaper print processes, but equally as important in the distribution and marketing of the work. The internet, simple-to-use blogs, PayPal and Twitter have allowed us to promote and display work to an international audience and removed the need to work with distributors. This is a topic I hope we can discuss further; I'd be very interested to hear your thoughts about the role digital technology is playing beyond the photographic capture and work production stage.

Perec has been very influential on my practice, most definitely. The first book I read by Perec is titled *Species of Spaces and Other Pieces*[10] and is essentially a collection of some of his shorter texts.

The work of Perec's that I find particularly relevant are essays such as, *Species of Spaces*, *Notes on the Objects to be Found on my Desk*[11] and *Brief Notes of the Art and Craft of Sorting Books.*[12] These three texts all focus on relatively mundane subject matter but apply an analytical observation process and it is this concept of the 'work' being the record of the 'process' that particularly interests me. With all the work that I produce, I am by no means saying that this is the end; the outcome is simply a record of the process that I went through to take the photographs and hopefully it provokes some readers to carry out a similar activity themselves. I feel that a lot of photography can make a viewer quite passive, in the sense that now they have a book of, for example, landscape photographs, that they do not then need to go out to a natural landscape. I hope that my work gives the audience a sense of process, but that it also frustrates them in a way so they want to see more. The only way then to see more is to go out and actually explore themselves.

Anyway, that's enough from me.
Look forward to hearing your thoughts about some of these topics.
Adam

From: Diane Smyth
To: Adam Murray
Sent: Tue, Mar 20, 2012 at 5.53pm
Subject: Preston, Paris, Process

I know what you mean re the photofairs, they can be a mixed bag. I think the fair which took place over *Paris Photo* last year, *Off Print*[13], was interesting in that it showed the sheer size of the small and self-published book world now – it was almost too much to take in, there was so much there. Perhaps as a reaction to that, and to the patchy quality you've touched on, I've enjoyed some of the events which are aimed at being exhibitions rather than fairs. The exhibition staged at *Le Garage*[14] at the Arles photofestival last year was still sizeable but it picked out some of the more interesting photobooks to have surfaced in the previous year, and personally I felt freer to flip through the books without feeling awkward about buying anything or not. On the other hand, it's nice to have the opportunity to talk with the photographers and artists who have put these books together, to get more idea of what they're aiming to do.

The recent exhibition at the ICA on serial publications[15] was really interesting from that point of view, in that it picked out particular books but gave quite a lot of detail about what they were trying to say and the context in which they were made; I also appreciated the fact that it reunited the photobook with the long history of artists' books. On the other hand, it was a shame not to be able to flip through the publications, which were exhibited safely behind glass because they're so rare. I think this is a practical issue that galleries have yet to resolve – the exhibition of Latin American photobooks at *Le Bal*[16], Paris is fascinating, for example, but it too has a problem in that it can't let visitors leaf through books for themselves. It tries various strategies to show the books off, including putting them behind glass, blowing up copies of the spreads and showing videos of flicking through the books, but none of these replicates the experience of having a look through for yourself. It will be interesting to see how Tate Modern handles this question in October at the *Klein/Moriyama* show[17], as both photographers are famous for the use of the photobook format.

I guess this is where the accessibility of your books comes in – not only are they available and affordable, their lo-fi construction means that they're approachable too. Jason and Benedict have a point re the limited editions but then it only goes to show that the apparently infinite reproducibility of photography is always bounded by practical concerns – even using cheap photocopiers, you can only print off so many books at one time. I think it's a function of the physicality of books – they exist in the world, therefore they have a finite number and existence. If you look at it that way, even mass-market newspapers like *The Sun* are limited editions, it's just that the edition is enormous. On the other hand, you could print more books as and when requested, so I wondered why have you opted not to do so. Does creating new copies beyond the first print run make such a difference to the images? I think Benedict is right re the limited edition too – in numbering the books you do rarify each copy – why have you opted to do so?

Digital publishing does offer a way around all this as, once you've made a PDF, it's up to the viewer whether to view it, or even print it. It's like being given the ability to put a transparency in every viewer's hands, and I know that's something that you're excited about doing. In fact, I was impressed to see you guys put out an app[18], long before most photographers started to experiment with this format. In this case you're not in control of the 'edition' and the idea of the edition may not even be appropriate – but even still, the physical world will impinge on how the images are distributed. iPads and iPhones are pretty expensive and way beyond the means of many in the UK, let alone outside the Western world. This may all change in the future but for the moment, I think your photobooks are probably more accessible if they're printed. Added to that, when you print a photobook you have the opportunity to put it in front of people in their day-to-day life, whereas with iPad or iPhone apps people have to seek out and download your app. As you mention too, there are a lot of images online and it can be difficult to get traction that way – although the internet can also afford ways to reach a lot of people via Twitter *et al*. The problem with Twitter and Facebook is that they tend to speak to small communities though (for example to your 'fans'), and blogs are similar. Have you found this a problem? How do you use the internet to speak to people beyond the photography community?

Your comments re Perec are interesting – the idea that it is the 'process' that is interesting, rather than the end result – it's appropriate that we're putting together an essay using the 'process' of these emails rather than a finished essay. But, other than by using everyday subject matter and means of reproduction, how are you encouraging other people to make photobooks? Have you been tempted to work with people somehow to help them make images? Or do you think there are problems with the participatory photography model? And have you been tempted to show more of your 'workings' in your photobooks? For example, some of the ways and means in which you shoot? For example, Perec is charmingly honest about the difficulties of watching everyday life in his Saint-Sulpice work, and allows his text to break down to show some of these problems.

Thanks

Di

From: Adam Murray
To: Diane Smyth
Sent: Thu, Mar 22, 2012 at 4.22pm
Subject: Preston, Paris, Process

Hello Di
It's interesting that you mention about the different major bookfairs/exhibitions that you've been to and the different experiences of each. For me the ICA show was a real disappointment as an exhibition. I completely agree with you about the high quality of curation and how interesting the work on display was and the contextual information; but all of this and more is contained in the book that accompanies the show, however this does cost £50 whereas entry to the exhibition is free.

As a separate area of research to this discussion, I have been thinking about investigating what the purpose of the 'book exhibition' is and whether there is a more effective way of bringing artists' and photographers' books into the public realm beyond a gallery or book shop. A couple of weeks ago I was talking with Eleanor Brown who runs *X Marks the Bökship*[19] in East London and she showed me an interesting body of work called

Open Books[20] edited by Charlotte Cheetham and Sophie Demay. The publication is a collection of texts that discuss books as exhibited material so I'm looking forward to getting chance to read this. What are your thoughts about this?

One of the best recent experiences I have had with a photobooks is taking a group of undergraduate students from the University of Central Lancashire, where I am a lecturer, to visit the Artists' Book Special Collection at Manchester Metropolitan University.[21] The senior library assistant, Jane Pendlebury, had selected a range of books that the students were free to look through. The library operates almost an open door policy where people can go in and look through the collection; it is a wonderful resource for actually physically engaging with the books. One thing that I think would be great for the *Klein/Moriyama* show is to get a large number of facsimile copies made of their key books and have a 'library' set up in one of the Tate Modern rooms where visitors can spend time looking through these near perfect copy versions, but I imagine this would require a significant budget and management.

Moving back to *Preston is my Paris* and another thing I am finding really useful about our conversation is that it is really making me ask questions about my practice. I suppose that the numbering thing was quite naïve to begin with and this was just the thing to do, but now I think about it more, it is definitely something I would consider addressing in the future. I have made a conscious decision not to reprint or do second editions of publications though and this is something I do not think would change. This relates to the subject matter of the work in the sense that each publication is trying to raise the *now* in the consciousness of the audience, encouraging them to explore and engage with the moment before it is gone. So once each publication has sold out, this is the chance missed.

I am definitely aware of the small community problem that can occur with work of this nature and there is a small group of people that always buys the publications and that I meet at book fairs and exhibitions. This is by no means a bad thing, and I am very grateful to people such as yourself, Bruno Ceschel,[22] Martin Parr, Jason Evans, Conor Donlon[23] and Eleanor who have supported the work from the outset and also the collectors, but I am actively trying to get the work out to a mass audience and consequently show the 'workings' of the projects.

The internet helps with this, but the method I have been experimenting with more is live events. Since early 2010 Robert and I have put on live projects and events in a diverse range of spaces such as a disused shop in an arcade in Preston, the old National Express ticket office in Preston Bus Station, Phoenix Arts Centre in Brighton and Son Gallery in Peckham. Each venue has very different purposes and very different types of people who visit them, but they have all been helpful in terms of developing my understanding about the role photography can have in engaging with audiences.

Denim,[24] which you first featured in the *British Journal of Photography*, was a project that I collaborated with Jamie Hawkesworth on, the concept of which was to carry out a fashion shoot in the shopping arcade in Preston. We chose denim as the theme as Preston is twinned with Nimes in France where the fabric is reported to have originated, then over the weekend all the clothing was sourced in Preston and we scouted the models from the city as well. This included plumbers on their lunch break, teenagers and a group of mothers out with the children shopping on a Sunday and was a thoroughly enjoyable experience.

One criticism I have about my role in the project though was not maintaining the relationships with the participants, this is something I intend to address is future work. I remember you featured this in a fashion-themed issue of the *BJP*, what initially caught your attention about the work?

Towards the end of 2011 I devised a project titled *FIND*[25] which consisted of setting up a live project space in a gallery in Brighton and inviting residents of the city to contribute items and photographs to an archive of everyday life. Throughout the month of the project the collection grew and then at the end we printed a series of publications featuring the items live in the project space. Concept-wise I think this is one of the strongest bodies of work I have done, but in terms of engaging with a wide audience I was disappointed. The project simply did not attract a wide range of people and ended up really being made up of people that would visit the gallery normally. I think that there are a number of reasons for this happening, relating to type of venue, methods used to promote and raise awareness of the project and clarity about the purpose of the project. This is something I am looking to change in future projects, such as the current one I am working on with Sheffield-based photographer Theo Simpson.[26]

I know that you attend a number of live photographic events with your work. Are there any that have particularly stood out for you as having an innovative approach to working with audiences?

Speak soon

Adam

From: Diane Smyth
To: Adam Murray
Sent: Mon, Mar 26, 2012 at 5.38pm
Subject: Preston, Paris, Process

Hi Adam
Yes, I think I might agree with the sub-text of what you write – that a library of books, or even facsimiles of books, is a better way to show photobooks than trying to show them in exhibitions. I do understand the practical difficulties of doing so but exhibitions, which put the books behind glass, just give such a different experience. Ironically, reproducing series of images into photobooks turns them into objects, and mitigates against the idea of the photograph as infinitely reproducible image – I think the fact that you print a certain number of copies of your photobook and leave it at that neatly addresses this fact. Galleries aren't the only ones trying to find tactics to overcome this problem though, bookshops and book reviewers are also trying methods such as filming themselves turning the pages. As others have pointed out, photobooks seemed to often be filmed or photographed being fondled!

One solution that the publisher Michael Mack[27] has suggested is republishing classic photobooks as page-turning iPad apps. Obviously the tactile sensation of the book would be lost, but the personal control over the speed and direction in which the book was read could be returned – one of the downfalls of watching a film of someone else flipping through a photobook is that you don't have that control. You've mentioned creating *Preston Institute of the Everyday (PIE)*[28] PDFs, which the reader could freely download and then flick through at will. Is that something you're still thinking of doing? I think it could be interesting – again, it goes back to the idea of the infinitely reproducible image, and on a practical level allows you to distribute as many copies of the 'book' as are required at no extra cost. On the other hand, are page-turning apps or PDFs missing a trick? Digital imaging and the prevalence of computers and tablets allow photographers to do so much more with moving images and audio files, but should you feel obliged to do something with them? We're living through interesting times, in which the media we consume is evolving very quickly, and I think we are all only just beginning to play with what's possible. What do you think?

Your comments re live events are interesting – it seems to me that 'experiences' are now a big part of our culture, despite (or perhaps because) of the increasing amount of time we're all spending online and on our computers. I thought the Preston bus station project was really great – initially what attracted me was simply the quality of the images included in it, then when I found out more about it I was even more intrigued. I liked the egalitarian nature of it, the idea that any of the people you found in the bus station could be stylish and merit attention, rather than the supermodels and celebrities who seem to take up so much of our media now. Actually it reminded me of style magazine such as *The Face* or *i-D*, though, which started out by looking at street fashion. *The Face* is long gone and *i-D* is a high-fashion magazine now and I think that's a shame – I like the idea of bottom-up fashion, that might emerge from the street before being taken up further up, rather than the top-down idea that we are all passive consumers of fashion designed by others. I guess it's a DIY approach that links with Perec too – the idea that we can take control over how we look, rather than simply following what others decide. As such, I think it links with your project and what we're doing here – showing the process and trying to encourage others to take action, rather than passively consuming.

From that point of view, it's interesting that you tried to do a project where you gathered others' images – and that so few people responded. I guess with the best will in the world, not everyone will want to be creative – perhaps too, amateur photographers are more familiar with putting their images online than in galleries. Again, it could be that exhibitions aren't the best way to show this kind of work. The good thing about photography is that it's so egalitarian, particularly now that phones are so widespread, most people have the experience of taking photographs. These photographs may not be what the photography community considers good or interesting right now – that judgement might change though, and when so many people are taking so many images it's probably inevitable the images will become more sophisticated too. For me, it's interesting to see how photographers are starting to engage with amateurs' images – at the *From Here On* exhibition at *Les Rencontres d'Arles* in 2011 there were quite a few projects gathering together amateurs' images from the internet. Sometimes this seemed to include a rather snide power balance, though, in which the professional photographer poked fun at the naive images the mass had thrown up. Again I think that it's early days and perhaps too early to see where all this is going – apologies if this seems like a cop out, and even more of a cop-out, I will throw the topic back to you...

Thanks

Di

From: Adam Murray
To: Diane Smyth
Sent: Wed, Mar 28, 2012 at 10.50pm
Subject: Preston, Paris, Process

Hello Di
Yes, we are definitely going to do the PDF version of *PIE* still, planning on putting it online in the next couple of weeks. The reason for doing it as a PDF is exactly as you have said, you are able to distribute the work for free, but using the PDF format means that you don't need a specialised tool such as an iPad to view it on, just some form of computer. This will hopefully broaden the accessibility and then audiences can choose to view it in a variety of ways. This is also a multimedia project in that we worked with a colleague of mine, Rob Griffiths, to produce a sound piece that accompanies the photographic work. The theme of *PIE 1* is public transport so the sound piece is a collection of ambient sound recordings of public transport from different European cities. This has then been made into a podcast that can be downloaded for free from iTunes. This particular body of work has very much been influenced by earlier experiments with multimedia 'publications' such as *Aspen*[29] and the

Fluxus boxes, but digital technology now offers new opportunities for production and distribution.

I would agree that we are in a very exciting period of change and development, but the wonderful thing is that a range of practitioners is still exploring all this. What I am finding particularly interesting is that people are experimenting with a variety of approaches and are almost embracing the risk of failure. Rather than focusing on just the end product practitioners seem to not be afraid to work through the process of their work in the public realm. This transparent view then gives audiences a number of different points of enquiry for them to develop their own projects in response. Even if an audience is not so engaged with the final set of photographs, an element of the process may prove to be very inspirational.

For me, Nick Knight has been a pioneer of this with *SHOWstudio.*[30] By embracing new developments in technology, Knight has given mass audiences unprecedented access into the process of his work but also placed emphasis on how significant this process can be. Another recent body of work that I feel fits this concept is the *Postcards From America*[31] project produced by some Magnum photographers. Although I am aware that the final outcome has received a mixed response, seeing such a significant and respected photographic organisation embrace blogs, social networking and user-generated content, is really very exciting.

In terms of whether photographers should feel obliged to use video, sound, web-based platforms etc. I think that the important thing to consider is the purpose of each project and choosing the appropriate medium and technology to realise this and not just to use a medium for the sake of it. Often it is easy to get seduced by new technology and move focus away from the content and value of the work and this is something that I am very keen to avoid with *Preston is my Paris*. In current photography there is still the need to embrace gallery-based outcomes, printed matter and digital formats, as long as the decisions are appropriate for the project. The joy of now is the amount of options that are available.
Adam

NOTES

1 http://www.prestonismyparis.blogspot.co.uk/ and http://www.pppbooks.blogspot.co.uk/

2 Book Arts Fayre took place at Ffotogallery, Cardiff, 25th–26th February 2012, http://www.ffotogallery.org/

3 B Book Show took place at Ground Floor Left, London, 2nd–4th March 2012, http://www.photobookshow.co.uk/

4 Released September 2010.

5 Released August 2010.

6 Georges Perec, *An Attempt at Exhausting a Place in Paris* (Adelaide: Wakefield Press, 2010)

7 Georges Perec, *Species of Spaces and Other Pieces* (London: Penguin, 2008) 210

8 Jason Evans *I am Julian Assange* (Brighton: Photoworks 2011) 80

9 Benedict Burbridge *Riot Scene* (London: Grafik 2011) 28-31

10 Georges Perec, *Species of Spaces and Other Pieces* (London: Penguin, 2008)

11 Georges Perec, *Thoughts of Sorts* (London: Notting Hill Editions, 2011) 9-15

12 Georges Perec, *Thoughts of Sorts* (London: Notting Hill Editions, 2011) 23-33

13 Off Print took place at 21-24 Rue Ganneron, Paris, 10th–13th November 2011

14 http://www.legarage.cc/

15 *In Numbers: Serial Publications by Artists Since 1955*, ICA, London, 25th January – 25th March 2012

16 *Foto Grafica: A New History of the Latin American Photobook*, Le Bal, Paris, 20th January – 8th April 2012

17 *William Klein/Daido Moriyama*, Tate Modern, London, 10th October 2012 – 20th January 2013

18 http://itunes.apple.com/au/app/preston-is-my-paris/id379576897?mt=8

19 http://bokship.org/

20 Charlotte Cheetham & Sophie Demay, *Open Books* (Paris: Association Catalyst, 2011)

21 http://www.specialcollections.mmu.ac.uk/

22 http://selfpublishbehappy.com/

23 http://www.donlonbooks.co.uk/

24 Released March 2010

25 http://findbrighton.blogspot.co.uk/

26 http://theosimpson.com/

27 http://www.mackbooks.co.uk/

28 PIE 1 released October 2011

29 Phyllis Johnson, *Aspen* (New York: Roaring Fork Press, 1965-71)

30 http://showstudio.com/

31 http://postcards.magnumphotos.com/

Imaginary Shadows: Fictional Documentary Photography in Artists' Books

SARAH BODMAN
Centre for Fine Print Research
University of the West of England
Bristol

Artists making books often use photography as a means of recording a narrative of place, journey, observations on travels, or to bring together collections of artefacts and present them as a coherent story. But what if artists use photography in the book format to document things that aren't actually there, things they missed or haven't done, or use photography to produce fake versions of other artists' books?

The following examples have been produced by artists who are interested in what we are missing, and what or who isn't there. Frans Baake's islands, never visited, only fleetingly glimpsed at a distance; Scott McCarney's disappearance of the physical evidence provided by photographs that prompt our memories; books that appropriate the seminal style and subject matter of Ed Ruscha's artists' books, yet have completely different contents; imagined character scenes from novels the artist is reading, produced in another place at another time as a series of impromptu, fictional stage sets. They can even be screen-based photographic books, in tribute to an artist's oeuvre, yet knowingly failing in their attempt to recreate the originals. Documenting the undocumentable, they cast their shadows in the field of photographic artists' books.

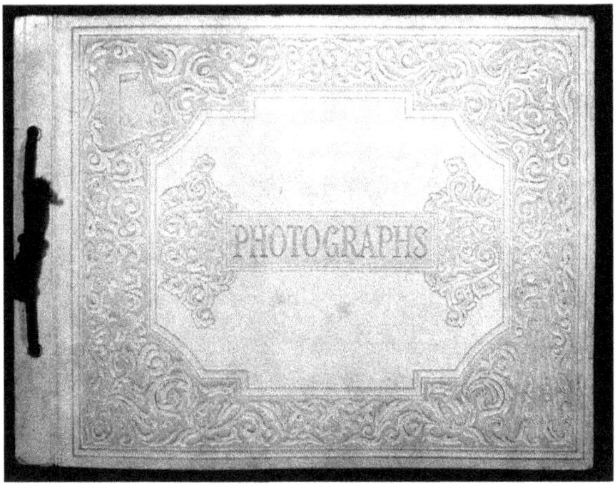

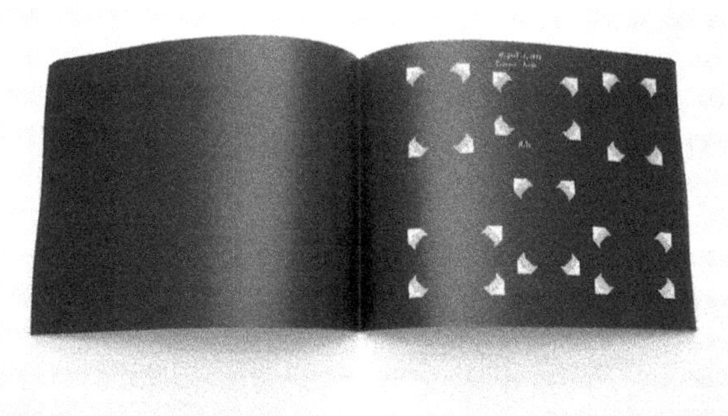

Photographs, *Scott McCarney, 2007.*

McCarney's *Photographs* (2007) is a book of absence, a book containing only what disappears over time: names, places, events are forgotten without the visual prompt to remind us of days out, family and friends, milestones documenting our lives. All we have left is our imagination to fill in the missing pieces, to try and build a story of what the album could represent for us.

A series of McCarney's artists' books which has been ongoing for 14 years, documents his autobiographical stories, from *Memory Loss* (1998) inspired by his brother's injuries, to *HELLO my name is SCOTT* (2006) which contains a collection of name badges he has been given at book fairs and related events. His collection of four *Autobiographies* (1999) lays bare a series of minutiae from his life; maps drawn for him to aid his travels; rejection letters from applications spanning twenty years; to do lists; photographs of the artist alongside famous people. His *C(a[e{I}o]u)P: Autobiography #5* (2005) is a double layout book. The interior photographs document McCarney's postcards to his parents interspersed with images of his father's collection of home-recorded videotapes printed over handwritten to do lists in one book; more postcards with his collection of baseball caps and his mother's tea cups in another. All gathered from boxes unpacked after McCarney's parents had died:

> *"Collections are autobiographies that reflect the collector and the act of collecting as much as the objects collected. As I get older, the relationship between collecting and discarding parallels that of remembering and forgetting: I remember less and accumulate more."* [1]

Photographs is the one book in McCarney's output of more than 40 editions that tells us nothing, it represents all that gets slowly lost, and it becomes even more poignant when viewed alongside his memory-packed collections of the rest of his life to date.

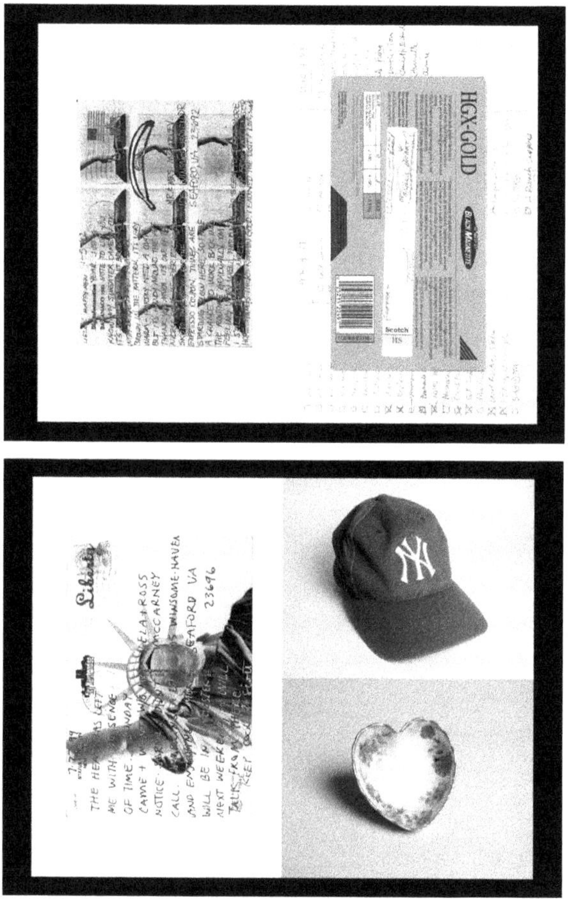

C(a[e{l}o]u)P: Autobiography # 5, Scott McCarney, 2005.

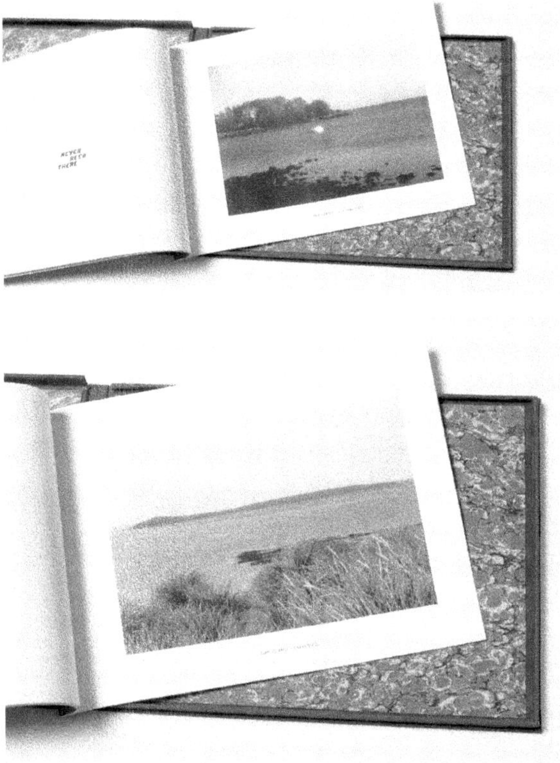

Never been there, *Frans Baake, The Netherlands, 2004. Photographs: Johan Ghijsels.*

Frans Baake has been travelling to islands with his camera for many years. From these travels he produces his own small editions of hand printed artists' books and has also written stories about his escapades for Dutch magazines including *Voyager.*

The more inaccessible the islands are, the more effort Baake will put it into almost getting to them, and the more inhospitable they are the more he will do to spend time on them, photographing in the mist, fog, wind and rain in order to produce a photograph that reveals almost nothing about the location. It's a perverse kind of travel documentary, producing artists' books that show the viewer the bleakness of the weather, or a glimpse of a speck of an island that cannot be reached.

Baake's recent works have also veered into rivers and islets: *Aits & Eyots* (2011) was produced, in a larger edition of 200, from a one-day visit to twelve unexpected islets in the River Thames near London. Baake was hopeful that he would be able to photograph each islet as he stepped upon it, but there were so many private islands that were inhabited by those not wishing to receive strangers that the book ranges from photographs of islands he actually set foot upon, to long-distance photographs of those he only noticed at a distance, and blanks for those that he could not set foot upon.

Never been there (2004) is a beautifully presented collection of islands that Baake has photographed from nearby or from a distance. As he says, "the artist has been to the specific regions in order to say that he hasn't been there: wow, how many places he didn't visit!" [2]

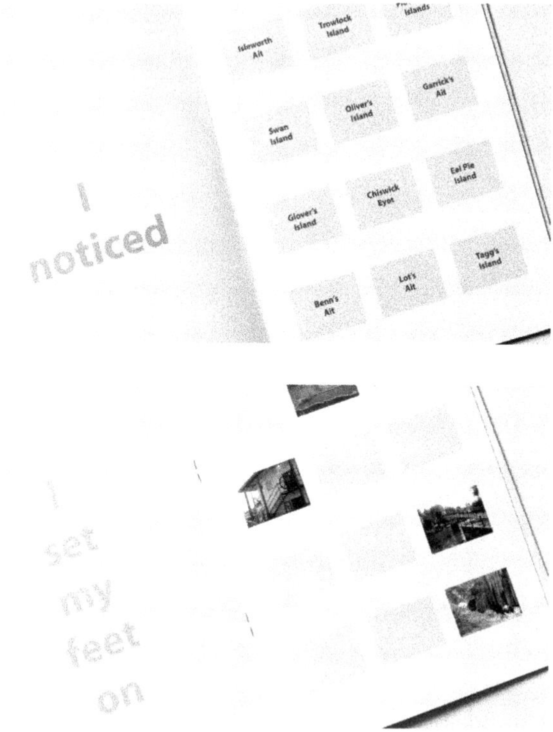

Aits & Eyots, *Frans Baake, The Netherlands, 2011. Photographs: Johan Ghijsels.*

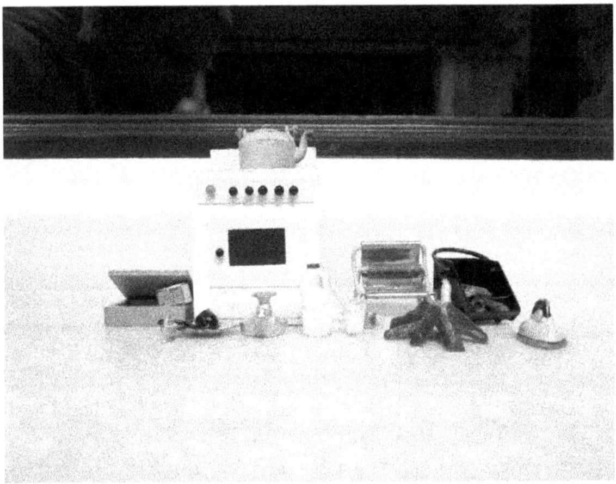

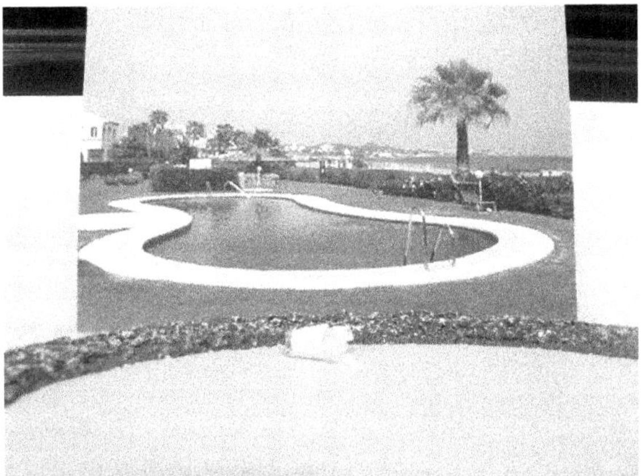

No Dutch Details, *Tom Sowden and Sarah Bodman, 2011.*

No Dutch Details is a photographic, screen-based tribute to Ed Ruscha's *Dutch Details* (1971). Tom Sowden and I produced *No Dutch Details* on an intercity train from Amsterdam Schiphol to Enschede, The Netherlands (stopping at Deventer) between 19.47 and 20.00 on Sunday 16 January 2011.

The format replicates the incremental zoom-in to close-up image layout in Ruscha's *Dutch Details*, as a 21st century, screen-based, chronological tribute to all of his books published between 1963 and 1978. Each of original books was recreated using only props found or created in miniature that could be balanced on a small tray-table in order to be photographed on the train. *No Dutch Details* deliberately fails to create a faithful reproduction of any of Ruscha's books, as the titles of each section in the tribute indicate.[3]

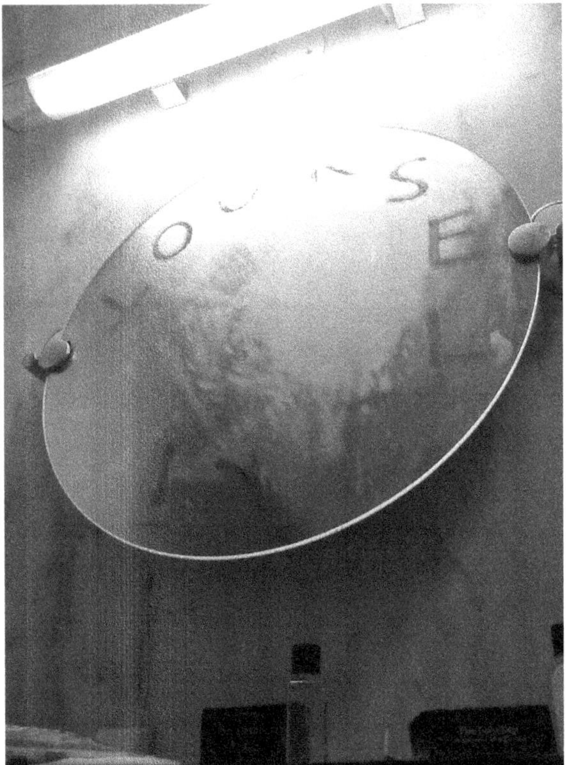

Flowers in Hotel Rooms Volume IV, *Sarah Bodman, 2009.*

Flowers in Hotel Rooms is an ongoing series of pocket-sized artists' books made in tribute to characters in the novels I read when I travel, but these aren't real events. They involve an impromptu stage set and camera, depending on the book's content and what I can find to produce a postcard-sized image in a hotel room.

I always make sure I have a book with me when travelling, and have spent many hours reading in hotel rooms good and bad whilst working away from home. I never paid much attention to what I was reading in relation to where I was staying until, in 2002 whilst at the Frans Masereel Centrum in Belgium, I started to read Richard Brautigan's novel, *The Abortion: An Historical Romance 1966* (1971), which includes a character who has written a book on growing flowers in hotel rooms by candlelight. The image this conjured up in my mind was so intriguing that I got to work straight away on assembling candles and flowers to photograph in my room.

The series has continued to evolve ever since that moment in Belgium, as a set of journals, documenting my own actions in place of characters in novels, or writers whose work I admire. Working in Enschede in The

Netherlands I asked to stay in room 451, so I could make my complicated tribute to Ray Bradbury; burning a paper flower for Guy Montag (whilst reading Edgar Allen Poe's *Tales of Mystery and Imagination*). In Glasgow, reading Chuck Palahniuk's *Survivor* I amused myself in Palahniuk fashion by asking a friend if he could write "kill yourself" in the steam on the bathroom mirror of the hotel room he was sharing with another friend of ours, who is never fully awake in the mornings, and of course he didn't notice it.[4]

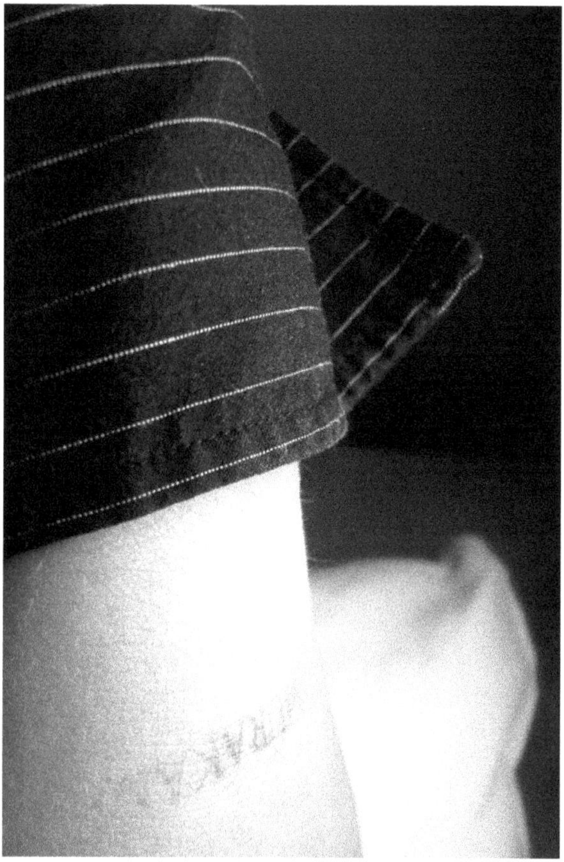

Flowers in Hotel Rooms Volume IV, *Sarah Bodman, 2009.*

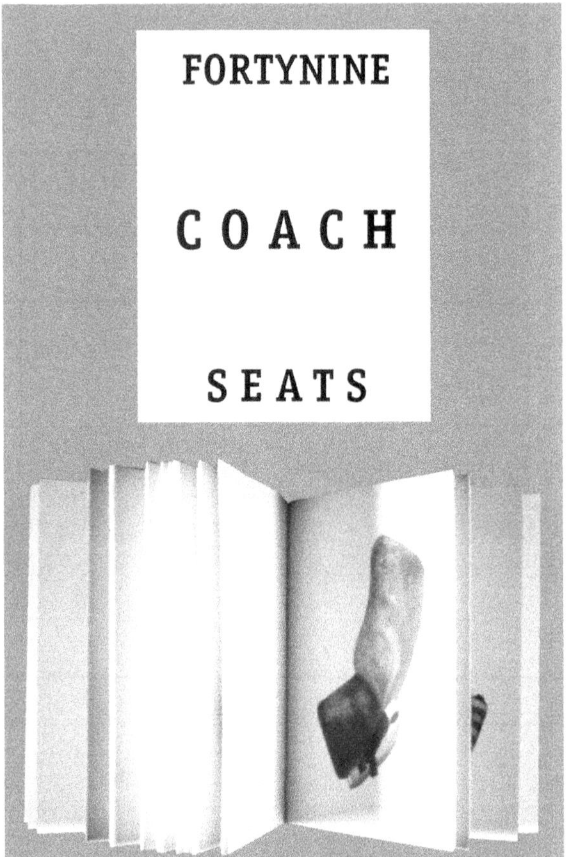

Fortynine Coach Seats Travelling Along the M4, *Tom Sowden, 2003.*

Tom Sowden has been making artists' books in the style of Ed Ruscha since 2003, when he was introduced to Ruscha's work as "the godfather" of contemporary artists' books. At that time Sowden was living in Bristol and studying in London. His commute to college took hours, the majority of which was spent in a coach on the motorway. Six hours a week was time he felt that he could use to produce books about the journey. Sowden was also reading *Non-Places: Introduction to an Anthropology of Supermodernity* by the French anthropologist Marc Augé, who described exactly the kind of space Sowden found himself in a "non-place".

The combination of repeated travel on the motorway, discovering Augé's writings and his exposure to the books of Ed Ruscha began Sowden's engagement with non-place and his first homage to Ruscha. Each time Sowden boarded the coach, he recorded a photograph of the seat that he would then occupy, and so, *Twentysix Gasoline Stations*, turned into *Fortynine Coach Seats Travelling Along the M4*. Presented in chronological order (with gaps where he couldn't take a picture of the seat, echoing Ruscha's blank pages) and cut from their surroundings with no explanation, the seats take on their own characters. Forty-nine is the standard number of seats on a National Express coach and, keeping as true to Ruscha's work as possible, Sowden used a similar typeface and font size, as a tongue-in-cheek reference that reflected the humour of Ruscha's original.[5]

NOTES

1 Scott McCarney, *C(a[e{I}o]u)P: Autobiography #5* (New York: VSW Press, 2005), 2. Scott McCarney's artists' books can be viewed on his website: http://scottmccarneyvisualbooks.com/
A catalogue of McCarney's publications and multiples to date, produced for a solo exhibition in 2011, can be viewed at: http://issuu.com/smartbooks/docs/visualbooks

2 Frans Baake, "Never been there", in the *Artist's Book Yearbook 2006-2007* (Bristol: Impact Press, 2005), 132. For information on Frans Baake and his artists' books, see: www.fransbaake.nl

3 Ed Ruscha's *Dutch Details* was produced and published in Deventer, The Netherlands, by Stichting Octopus/Sonsbeek 71, in 1971. *No Dutch Details* contains the following sections: 2.6 Gasoline Stations; Various small fires and a carton and glass of milk; A building that could be a Los Angeles apartment block; Every building we could find, but not on the Sunset Strip; 3 or 4 parking lots in Los Angeles; Royal (plastic) Road Test; No Business Cards;
2 Swimming Pools and a broken glass (of milk); Some stains: tea, coffee, blood and tears; Crackers; Babycakes without weights; Real Estate Opportunities from the Internet; A Few Palm Trees; Records; Colored People and chewing gum; A bit of Hard Light, and can be viewed online at: www.bookarts.uwe.ac.uk/nodutchc.htm

4 The full series of *Flowers in Hotel Rooms* can be viewed at: http://www.bookarts.uwe.ac.uk/saragal.htm

5 Tom Sowden is co-curator, with Michalis Pichler, of the touring artists' books exhibition *Follow-Ed (after Hokusai)*. His artists' books can be viewed on his website: www.tomsowden.com

Reinstating Touch in the Documentary Photobook

TIM DALY
University of Chester

Interest in the authored documentary photography book form has increased exponentially since the publication of Andrew Roth's *The Book of 101 Books: Seminal Photographic Books of the Twentieth Century* (2001) and Martin Parr and Gerry Badger's *The Photobook: A History* (2004). Assisted by the emerging technology of on-demand printing and web-based distribution networks, as offered by Blurb.com and others, photographers can now self-publish for a hundredth of the costs incurred ten years ago. While the interaction between image, text and design on the printed page projects a scenario for the reader unavailable from the photograph alone, many documentary photobooks are variations on three book forms already established by the end of the 19th century: the album, the portfolio and the catalogue. Less common are those exploring the self-reflexive nature of the book, together with the unique materiality of the photographic print, such as Stephen Gill's *Warming Down* (2008) and fewer still use the medium's innate material qualities of light sensitivity and transience together with its unique sensory properties where a reading of the work is dependent on physical handling and material interaction.

Documentary photography, forever linked with

observational gathering and perceived by Roland Barthes as "a mechanical analogue of reality" (2000 [1956]: 197), has often been viewed as a second-tier practice, trapped between indexical and fictional representation. Jacob Riis' *How the Other Half Lives* (1890) established the early documentary book genre as a hybrid textual form combining factual narrative and indexical photographs albeit in a closed narrative loop, which as William Stott observes, "make the reader feel he is first-hand witness to a social condition" (1973: 214). Yet, as Jeff Allred proposes, later modernist documentary photobooks were more open ended. They "do not naturalize the social status-quo they index in word and image. Rather, they engage in a speculative practice of aesthetic construction... one that recruits readers in a shared project of thinking through plausible pasts, presents and futures." (2010: 7) Riis' book forefronted facts gleaned from the city's own health and housing census data with thirty unstaged, awkward photographs further evidencing his findings. Riis had neither the skills nor pretensions of a pictorialist and his raw, unmediated images were read as equivalents of reality. While Riis' book heralded the dawn of the mass-produced photobook, through the commercial possibilities offered by the new halftone printing process developed a few years earlier, it signalled the beginning of the end for the silver-based photographic print as a method of photo-mechanical reproduction in the book form. *How the Other Half Lives* paved the way for many documentary photography books of the 1930s. The potency of the form was tempting and, in later works, Riis repurposed his material into sentimental memoirs, endlessly cannibalising and recycling his own material to reach a wider audience.

Our encounter with the photobook form has a greater connection with our experience of reading and our expectations of received literary genres than any other visual art experience. Steven McCaffrey suggests we have two kinds of response to a book: "The physical experience of print as word and ink and the book itself as a physical object [plus] the psychological and psychosemantic experience of operating verbal signs." (2000 [1992]: 17) Karl Young suggests that the physical act of reading stimulates both inner speech and sight (2000 [1984]). Text in books act as a surrogate for oral activity and both acts of notation and reading are essentially performative. For many, reading is fast becoming separated from its physical origins and has become a perfunctory acquisition of data. With the prevalence of mass-market titles, where content matters more than form, the book as a physical entity has become a secondary carrier rather than a primary object.

Yet the history of photography itself is inextricably linked to the revolution brought about by mass-printing and, according to William Henry Fox Talbot, was first developed as a means of patenting the mass production of photographically illustrated books, not as a vernacular mass-market medium. Richard Benson, the master print technician responsible for the platemaking for many celebrated photographic books, has speculated that "photography was invented because the printing presses of the world needed more data than the hand could provide" (2008: 230), so as a by-product of the commercial halftone process in the late 1870s, the photobook demanded a very different kind of reading. As observed by Carol Armstrong, "the history of art largely removed the photograph from its printed and published context" (1998: 25) perhaps because of its very transparency. Yet the sequential deployment of images in a book delivered a more complex message than any individual, indexical print had managed up to that point.

Suffering from similar temptations of a commercial return, Margaret Bourke-White and Erskine Caldwell's *You Have Seen Their Faces* (1937) is the high-water mark of editorial intervention presented as factual documentary. While Bourke-White immortalised depression-era tenant farmers with a newly-acquired heroic modernist style (developed on assignment in Russia), Caldwell simply fabricated captions, falsely ventriloquising the depicted. Caldwell's preface clearly delineates his intended obfuscation:

> *The legends under the pictures are intended to express the authors' own conceptions of the sentiments of the individuals portrayed; they do not pretend to reproduce the actual sentiments of these persons.* (Caldwell, 1937)

The book form was used by post-war photographers as a way of legitimising their practice as art and to differentiate this form of photography from their commercial assignment work. Robert Frank, William Klein and Richard Avedon, together with designer Alexei Brodovitch, all asserted their status as artists by using the photobook form and symbolised their passage to professional recognition, without the expectation of financial reward. The link between photography and literature, however, is all-pervasive. Clement Greenberg infamously situated the work of Edward Weston within a modernist tradition, where the descriptive properties of his photographs place him "closer today to literature than the graphic arts" (1988 [1946]: 63). From pictorialism onwards, photographers' single iconic images borrowed readily from established literary traditions using metaphor, connotation and symbolism. Longer sequences of images planned as photobooks, described by Gerry Badger as "extended essays and literary novels" (2004: 8), also employ a uniquely visual form of storytelling. Walker Evans' *American Photographs* (1938) and Robert Adams' *Listening to the River* (1994) both display a form of visual syntax in the sequencing of the images or their juxtaposition within the double-page spread. Yet this framing of content originates not from a literary tradition but from the complementary and rhythmic hanging of fine prints on a gallery wall to facilitate our physical meandering through its three-dimensional space. Indeed, the sequencing plan of many photobooks is developed by physically walking past proof prints laid out in a studio setting, re-ordering their running, rehearsing the reader's experience and refining their, as yet unmade, journey.

Robert Frank's *The Americans* (1958) proposed an alternative visual syntax: a syncopated, gestural and stream-of-consciousness form, influenced by jazz, abstract expressionism and beat-generation literature. Suffocated by the constraints of commercial assignments, Frank instead bid for public sector funds to support his project, which was envisaged as a book from the outset, unlike many other photobooks of the preceding years, which were developed from repurposed content. Frank rejected the dominant photo-essay format, as used in *Picture Post* and *Life* magazines, which demanded a linear narrative with beginning, middle and ending, reacting to Roy Stryker's notion that the writing of a story and the narrative should precede the shoot (1986 [1946]). Frank deliberately left out more successful self-standing images in favour of weaker, gestural images in order to punctuate his sections and sequences with implied rhythms. Responses to

Frank's unconventional sequencing were mixed at the time; as John Szarkowski later recalled, "There was something almost offhand, a little kind of syncopated carelessness, a kind of foot-dragging rhythm to it." (2011 [1992]: 52) Caroline Blinder suggests that Frank's literary photography in *The Americans* "creates space for memory, to facilitate a form of storytelling [and] no matter how hard the photographer tries not to have a message, narratives and agendas occur." (2005: 117)

While Robert Frank's *The Americans* is physically located within the codex tradition, its intent and anti-linearity places it closer to an artist's book. As Simon Cutts advocates, "the [artist's book] is its own continuous accumulative impression, varying and differing not only for each reader, but each time it is read. For this continuous structure to be effective it must be the antithesis of a sequential reading." (2007: 172) Many documentary photography books, however, remain rooted in the *livre d'artiste* tradition – a more affordable form for aspiring art owners, developed by Skira and Tériades amongst others at the start of the twentieth century. This form of promotional book delivers a reproduction of artwork that exists elsewhere in a more auratic and desirable version.

The most lauded of all documentary photography books, Henri Cartier Bresson's *Images a la Sauvette* (1952) was not only issued by Tériades, (the publisher of *Jazz*, the 1947 *livre d'artiste* by Henri Matisse), but projected its very artistic intent by using a cover illustration by Matisse himself. Championed by 20th century photographers and publishers, books such as Josef Koudelka's *Gypsies* (1975), echo the idea suggested by Johanna Drucker that rarely do such titles interrogate the conceptual or material form of the book as part of its intention or thematic interests. (2004: 161)

The terrain of artist's books, however provides greater breadth for practice. As Simon Cutts advocated, "Artist-led publications attempt to synthesise text, image, material, method of production and context into a unified single work. When this succeeds, the book functions as a primary form." (2007: 47) Artist's books are made to be looked at and touched as well as read, providing a conceptual space and territory for all political, visual and textual transformations, collaborations and explorations. (Cotter 2004) Despite Drucker's depressing projection of the artist's book as "a mute space for unrealizable dreams" (2004: 363) many authored photography books celebrate thing-ness, self-reflexivity and independence.

The document within the terrain of artist's books extends across many different modes of practice, including performance documentation such as Ed Ruscha's *Royal Road Test* (1967) and Brian Lane's *Fog Log* (1978); the playing out of a concept or system such as Sol LeWitt's *Autobiography* (1980) and *Photogrids* (1977); or the collection and reframing of found or archive matter, such as Christian Boltanski's *Inventaire* (1973-98) series. The reproduced archive document is now most evident in the form of the facsimile book, which has taken a foothold in publishers' photography lists. With its not-for-publication origin, the facsimile promises an auratic, but ultimately voyeuristic experience. Facsimiles now include diaries, family albums, dummy books, sketchbooks, notebooks, contact prints, lost boxes, all manner of containers (including Mexican suitcases) and original out-of-print photobooks. The facsimile of Hans Peter Feldmann's *Album* (2008), is no more than a photographic ephemera version of Owen Jones' *The Grammar of Ornament* (1856). Unindexed and without text, it presents Feldmann's panoramic visual interests side-by-side, yet the form does nothing to illuminate Feldmann's idiosyncratic approach. Facsimiles allow us to be privy to the artist's raw thinking materials – they serve as a study-notes equivalent, coaching a richer interpretation from the original work.

The use of handwritten annotation in documentary photography books does much to reclaim the photographers' voice, which is traditionally submerged in the silent practice of photography. Bill Burke's *I Want to Take Picture* (1987) and Boris Mikhailov's *Look at Me I Look at Water* (2004) both combine handwritten notation alongside their images, projecting a highly personalised and existential interpretation. Jim Goldberg's *Open See* (2009), however, uses the handwritten annotations of the people he photographs on his prints. Like the handwritten ephemera celebrated in *Found*[1] magazine, Goldberg's image/text fusion combines the curious accent of the vernacular hand with their own image to create a voice mostly absent from these publications – that of the documented. As Batchen observes, "Even when prosaic in content, handwritten inscriptions suggest the voice of the writer, adding sound to the senses of touch and sight already engaged." (2004: 47)

The posthumously-published facsimile of

Kiyoshi Suzuki's *Soul and Soul* (2008) is a photobook that celebrates not the original book through the reprint process, but the photographer's own book dummy. What we have is an intriguing volume, richly marked and handled, perhaps in itself an additional document to the photographer's struggle to get published. The notion of the photographic document was further interrogated within the field of multiple art, networked art and independent publishing, under the influence of socialist ideology, emerging technology, alternative distribution and artist collaboration. The photographic multiples issued by Marcel Broodthaers, Ed Ruscha and Dieter Roth disrupt our received expectation of fine photographic reproduction descended from the dizzy heights of Edward Curtis' *North American Indians* (1907-30) and Alfred Stieglitz's *Camera Works* (1902-17) by using basic single colour offset, coarse halftones or colour photocopier. While the focus of networked art, as described by Jeanne Marie Kusina "is not the manner of [its] production, but the dynamic way in which [it is] distributed through artists' networks" (2005: 1), many independently published serials and zines delivered a new visual lexicon developed by the use of cheap and craft-free reprographic processes, celebrating touch, intervention and the sign of the maker's hand.

Despite the infinite reprographic potential of the photographic print, all but a few documentary photography books are constructed using lithography. By duplicating an already reprographic-capable medium, this method of distributing content disconnects the reader from the photographer's primary output. What Sontag described as "stenciled off the real" (1977: 154) becomes a copy of the stencil off the real. Lithography facilitates the distribution of the idea, but strips the photograph of its object status and wipes away the fingerprints of the creator, as found in annotated photographic prints and vernacular photo albums. As Verna Posever Curtis observes "[the photo album] felt the touch of both the original maker and its recipient" and "satisfies a shared human urge to touch and come in close contact with the representation of human experiences." (2011: 7) Alec Soth's *Las Vegas Birthday Book* (2008), printed with low-tech inkjet, alludes to more tactile, real-print experience.

Few artists use the material potential of the book to explore documentation, with Ed Ruscha's *Stains* (1969) being an exception. What *Stains* changes is the notion of the printed page as an empty signifier. Instead of being static, neutral and invisible, Ruscha's paper sheets are carriers of both object and image. Stephen Gill's *Buried* (2006) perhaps comes closest, compiling reproductions of his buried prints, with each book from the edition dipped in mud taken from the burial scene.

As access to image-making technology in developed societies has increased, the number of images we produce has become unimaginable, creating a dramatic change in our relationship with the photograph as object. Liz Jobey (2009) suggests that today, "images are manufactured, manipulated, recorded, broadcast, screened and stored. The nearest the human hand gets to them is the computer keyboard." Early photography, however, had a very different physical incarnation, and as Geoffrey Batchen observes, "It is as if... the subjects want to draw our attention not only to the image they hold, but also to photography itself as a touchable entity." (2004: 14) Daguerreotype cases with enclosed locks of hair, handwritten annotations, photo-jewellery operate as doubly indexical and heightened experiences of the subject. As Régis Durand speculates, they "allow me to believe that what is missing is present all the same, even though I know it is not the case." (2004 [1995]: 75-76)

I propose an alternative authored photography book: a super-sensory work, a document of participation, intervention and touch.[2] Echoing Batchen's words, these books can describe their documentary subjects "not as fixed and autonomous but as dynamic and collective, as a continual process of becoming." (2004: 97)

NOTES

1 See www.foundmagazine.com

2 My practice uses photography to document site/place/activity. However, the gathering of such images is fraught with the pitfalls of picturing elegiac redundancy and setting fluid, transient scenarios in a fixed, dead-end interpretation which stabilises and commodifies memory. In my practice, no single iconic image is sought; instead many smaller and disparate images are made on site, which then accrue a more complex narrative when viewed together as a sequence, or as an unfolding series of prints.
To fully explore the complexity of each subject, archive material developed by others is also included. In addition, discarded matter such as paper ephemera or textiles can be included, especially if it has the potential for becoming part of the book's contents, superstructure or packaging. By placing multiple indexical matter side-by-side, it is anticipated that the book will extend a linear representation of a site, by promoting a more complex end-user experience through a richer sensory interaction.

3 (See Figure 1) Harry Burton was the official photographer of the Tutankhamun tomb capturing the sequence of discovery, but also the imperial plunder and removal of artefacts from the tomb. The book idea was to narrate this episode with salted paper prints left unfixed on the page. From the time the seal is broken and the book opened, the images fade a little more, until they eventually fade to black. This inbuilt destruction – prompted by the very act of reading – creates an absurd dilemma for the viewer. Do they

continue to look at the unstable images on the page or do they keep the book closed?

4 (See Figure 2) Six unstitched King Penguin books altered with a single inkjet print placed in a vacant space on a double page spread. Each intervention makes an opportunistic connection with the book's original topic.

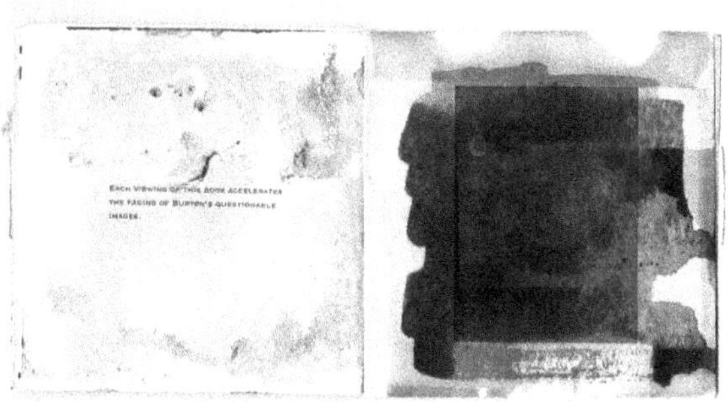

Figure 1: Returning Burton's Plunder. *Tim Daly (2010)* [3]
24pp silver nitrate/salt prints and inkjet on pulp paper, buckram cover with paper seal. Staple bound 140 x 140.

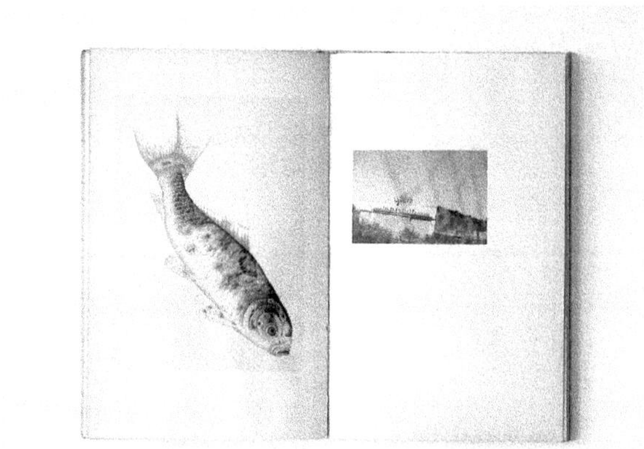

Figure 2: New Pocket Knowledge. *Tim Daly (2009)* [4]
Inkjet on altered King Penguin book. 300 x 205. Set of six.

References

Aarons, P., Roth, A (2009) *In Numbers: Serial Publications by Artists Since 1955*. Zurich: PPP Editions

Adams, R (1994). *Listening to the River.* New York: Aperture

Allred, J (2010) *American Modernism and Depression Documentary*. New York: OUP USA

Armstrong, C (1998) *Scenes in a Library: Reading the Photograph in the Book 1843-1875*. Cambridge: MIT Press.

Badger, G., and Parr, M (2004). *The Photobook: A history. Volume 1*. London: Phaidon Press

Barthes, R (2009) *Camera Lucida*. London: Vintage Classics

Batchen, G (2004). *Forget me not*. Amsterdam: Van Gogh Museum

Benson, R (2008) *The Printed Picture*. New York: MOMA

Blinder, C (2005) "Its beautiful visual entirety": Kerouac's introduction to Frank's The Americans (2005) in *Photography and literature in the twentieth century*. Cunningham Ed. Cambridge Scholars Press

Bourke-White, M & Caldwell, E (1937) *You Have Seen Their Faces*. New York: Modern Age

Burke, B (1987) *I Want to Take Picture*. New York: Nexus Press

Cartier Bresson, H (1952) *Images à la Sauvette*. Paris: Tériades

Cotter, H (2004) introduction to Drucker, J. *The Century of Artists' Books*. New York: Granary Books

Cutts, S (2007) *Some forms of availability: Critical passages on The Book and Publication*. Derby: RGAP

Day, J (2010). *Robert Frank's 'The Americans': The Art of Documentary Photography*. London: Intellect

Drucker, J (2004) *The Century of Artists' Books*. New York: Granary Books

Durand, R in Batchen, G (2004). *Forget me not*. Amsterdam: Van Gogh Museum

Evans, W (1938) *American Photographs*. New York: MOMA

Feldmann, HP (2008) *Album*. Berlin: Konig

Friedlander, Lee (1993) *Letters from the People*. London: Jonathan Cape

Frank, R (2008) *The Americans* (reprint). Goettingen: Steidl

Gill, S (2006) *Buried*. London: Nobody's Books

Goldberg, J. (2009) *Open See*. Goettingen: Steidl

Greenberg, C (1988) *The collected essays and criticism*.

Chicago: University of Chicago Press

Jobey, L (2009) Photographer Richard Benson: From the daggueroetype to the darkroom. In *The Guardian* 8th Jan 2009. Accessed March 20, 2102: http://www.guardian.co.uk/artanddesign/2009/jan/08/richard-benson-photography

Keller, U (1988) *The Highway as Habitat: A Roy Stryker documentation 1943-1955*. Santa Barbara: University Art Museum

Koudelka, J (1975) *Gypsies*. New York: Aperture

Kusina, JM (2005) The Evolution and Revolutions of the Networked Art Aesthetic. In *Contemporary Aesthetics*. Accessed March 20, 2102: http://www.contempaesthetics.org/newvolume/pages/article.php?articleID=263

LeWitt, S (1980) *Autobiography*. New York: Rizzoli

LeWitt, S (1977) *Photogrids*. New York: Rizzoli

Lane, B (1978) *Fog Log*. Self-published

Lyon, D (1968) *The Bikeriders*. New York: Macmillan

Mikhailov, B (2004) *Look at Me I look at Water*. Goettingen: Steidl

McCaffrey, Steven The Book as Machine. In *A Book of the Book*. New York: Granary Press

Posever Curtis, V (2011) *Photographic Memory: The album in the age of photography*. New York: Aperture/ Library of Congress

Riis, J (2001) *How the Other Half Lives*. London: Penguin

Ruscha, E (1967) *Royal Road Test*. Self-published

Stott, W (1973) *Documentary Expression and Thirties America*. Chicago: University of Chicago Press

Sander, A (1929) *Antlitz der Zeit*. Munich: Transmare Verlag

Sontag, S (1979) *On Photography*. London: Penguin

Suzuki, K (2008). *Soul and Soul*. Amsterdam: Aurora Borealis/Nordelicht

Szarkowski, J in Livingston, J (1992) *The New York School Photographs 1936-1963*. New York: Stewart, Tabori and Chang

Young, K. (1984) *Open Letter* pp 5-32

Memory of a Memory

LAWRENCE GEORGE GILES
University of Salford

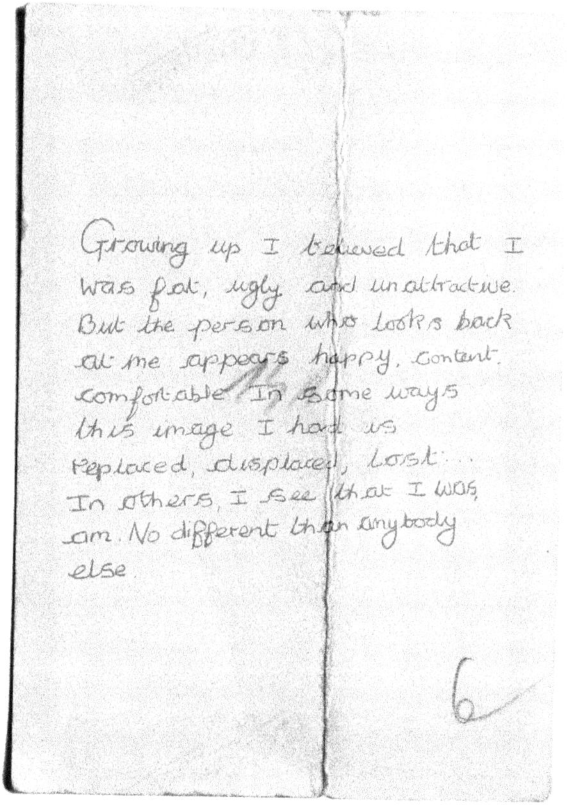

Growing up I believed that I
was fat, ugly and unattractive.
But the person who looks back
at me appears happy, content,
comfortable. In some ways
this image I had is
replaced, displaced, lost...
In others, I see that I was,
am. No different than anybody
else.

6

MY MUM IS LEANING AGAINST THE SIDE OF THE HOUSE
SHE HAS HER HANDS BEHIND HER BACK
SHE LOOKS SO YOUNG
I STILL SEE THAT IN HER AT TIMES

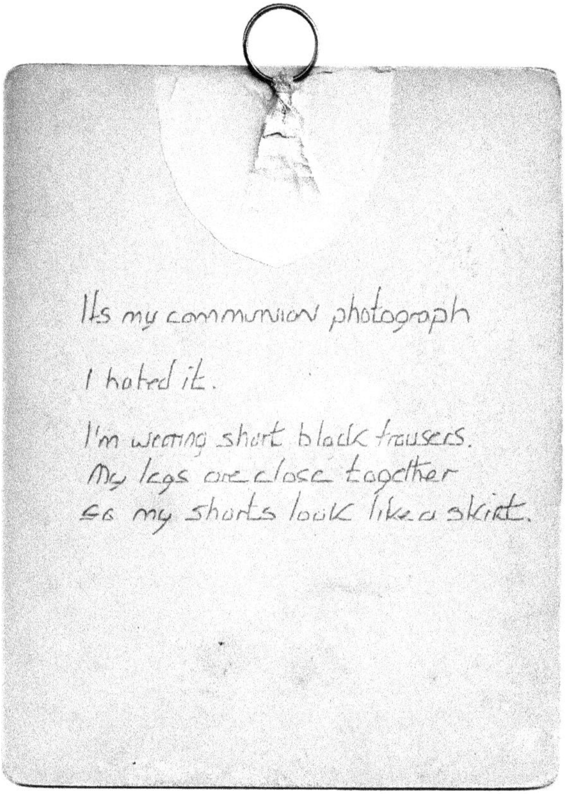
Its my communion photograph
I hated it.
I'm wearing short black trousers.
My legs are close together
so my shorts look like a skirt.

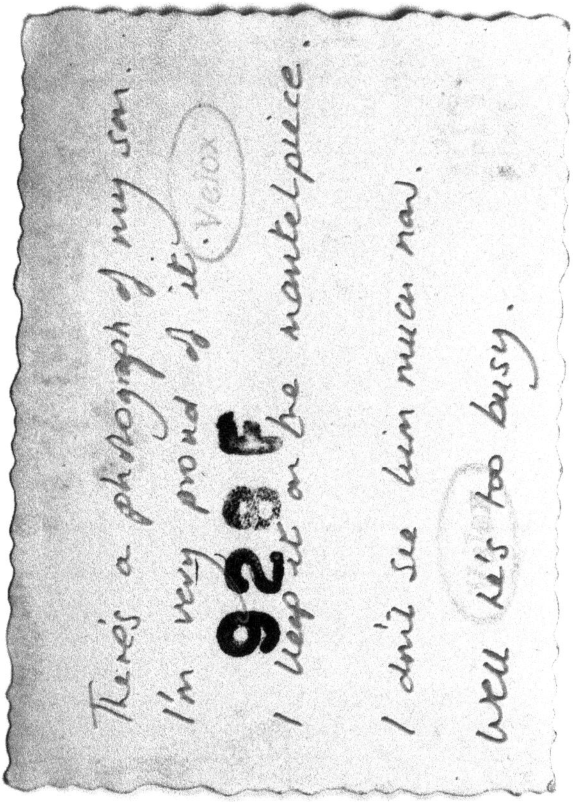
There's a photograph of my son.
I'm very proud of it.
I keep it on the mantelpiece.
I don't see him much now.
Well he's too busy.
Velox

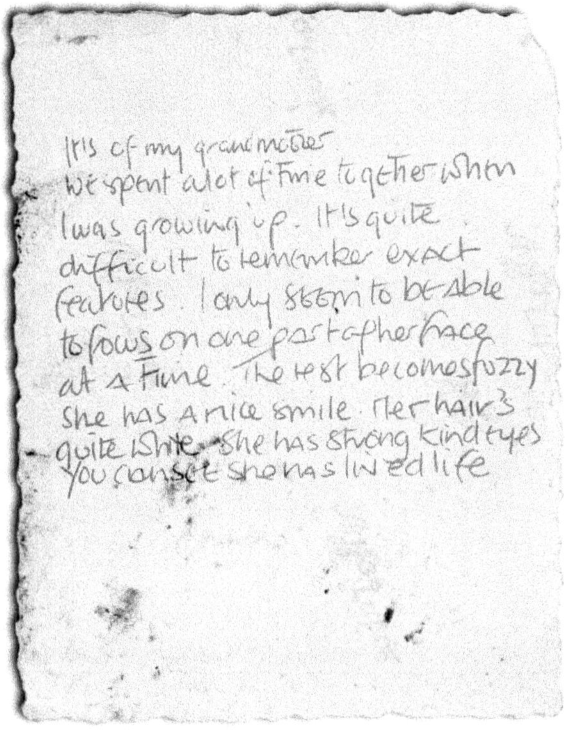
It's of my grandmother
We spent a lot of time together when
I was growing up. It's quite
difficult to remember exact
features. I only seem to be able
to focus on one part of her face
at a time. The rest becomes fuzzy
She has a nice smile. Her hair's
quite white. She has strong kind eyes
You can see she has lived life

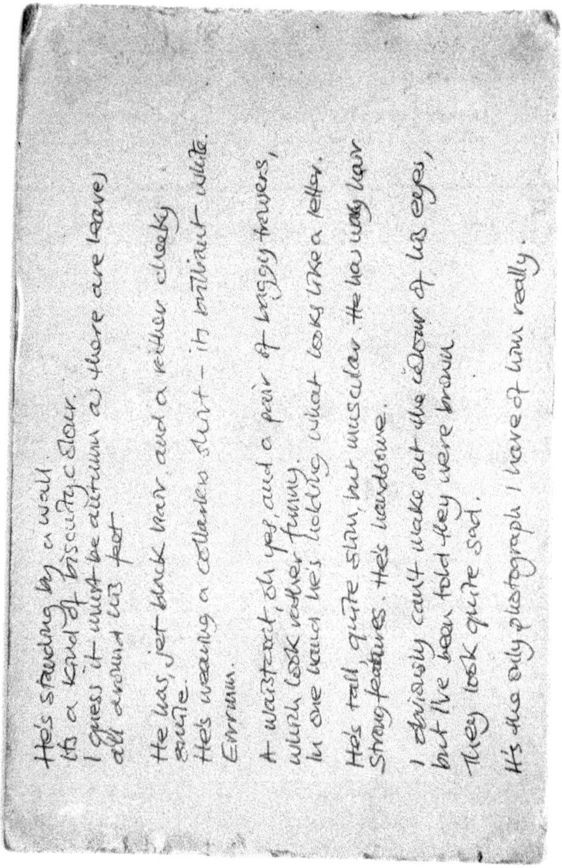

He's standing by a wall.
It's a kind of biscuity colour.
I guess it must be autumn as there are leaves
all around his feet.

He has jet black hair and a rather cheeky
smile.
He's wearing a collarless shirt – it's brilliant white.
Errmm.

A waistcoat, oh yes, and a pair of baggy trousers,
which look rather funny.
In one hand he's holding what looks like a letter.

He's tall, quite slim, but muscular. He has wavy hair.
Strong features. He's handsome.

I obviously can't make out the colour of his eyes,
but I've been told they were brown.
They look quite sad.

It's the only photograph I have of him really.

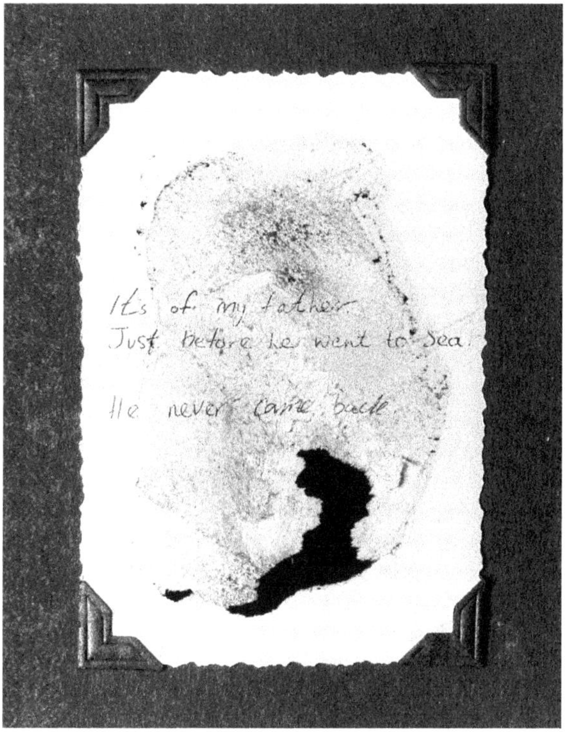
It's of my father
Just before he went to sea.
He never came back

About the Editors

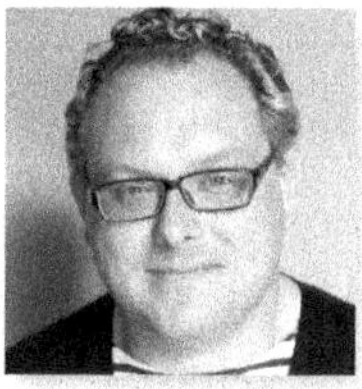

Jonathan Carson is one half of the creative partnership Carson & Miller. He and Rosie Miller have worked collaboratively as artists since 2000. Carson & Miller's practice is driven by their interest in narrative and the way in which they can tell and re-tell stories. Recent work has used the game, the book and the object as methodologies for collaboration and production.

Carson & Miller have produced a number of artists' books including *The Exquisite Fold* (2007, with Patricia Allmer and John Sears), *synopsis* (2008) and *Scrapbook (the story of things)* (2009, published by Manchester Metropolitan University Special Collections). In 2009, Carson & Miller edited the artists' book *stilled lives* for Righton Press. Artists' books by Carson & Miller have been acquired by a number of collections including Arts Council Ireland (Dublin), Chetham's Library (Manchester), Laurence Sterne Trust (Coxwold, Yorkshire), Limfjordscentret (Denmark) and Southern Cross University (Australia).

In 2009 Carson & Miller curated *The Story of Things* for Manchester Metropolitan University Special Collections (2009-2010). Other work has featured in exhibitions including *Swap/Vaihto* (UK & Finland, 2008) and *Universal Shipping Box* (Argentina, Germany and UK, 2010). Carson & Miller have played a series of games in galleries in Liverpool, Manchester and Berlin and have spoken and written about their work in a number of settings, including presentations in Belgium, the UK and the USA, and texts in publications including the journal *Image [&] Narrative* (2011) and *Recording Leisure Lives: Everyday Leisure in 20th Century Britain* (2012).

Jonathan Carson is Associate Head (Academic) and Senior Lecturer in Critical & Contextual Studies in the School of Art & Design, University of Salford, UK.

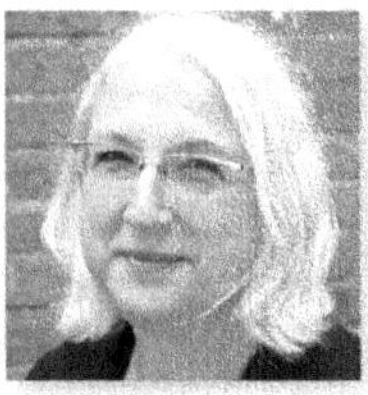
John Harding

Rosie Miller is one half of the creative partnership Carson & Miller. She and Jonathan Carson have worked collaboratively as artists since 2000. Carson & Miller's practice is driven by their interest in narrative and the way in which they can tell and re-tell stories. Recent work has used the game, the book and the object as methodologies for collaboration and production.

Carson & Miller have produced a number of artists' books including *The Exquisite Fold* (2007, with Patricia Allmer and John Sears), *synopsis* (2008) and *Scrapbook (the story of things)* (2009, published by Manchester Metropolitan University Special Collections). In 2009, Carson & Miller edited the artists' book *stilled lives* for Righton Press. Artists' books by Carson & Miller have been acquired by a number of collections including Arts Council Ireland (Dublin), Chetham's Library (Manchester), Laurence Sterne Trust (Coxwold, Yorkshire), Limfjordscentret (Denmark) and Southern Cross University (Australia).

In 2009 Carson & Miller curated *The Story of Things* for Manchester Metropolitan University Special Collections (2009-2010). Other work has featured in exhibitions including *Swap/Vaihto* (UK & Finland, 2008) and *Universal Shipping Box* (Argentina, Germany and UK, 2010). Carson & Miller have played a series of games in galleries in Liverpool, Manchester and Berlin and have spoken and written about their work in a number of settings, including presentations in Belgium, the UK and the USA, and texts in publications including the journal *Image [&] Narrative* (2011) and *Recording Leisure Lives:*

Everyday Leisure in 20th Century Britain (2012).

Rosie Miller is a Lecturer and Critical & Contextual Studies Area Leader in the School of Art & Design, University of Salford, UK.

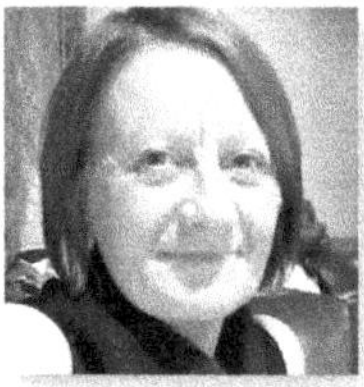

Theresa Wilkie works in the field of photography, with a particular interest in practice in the context of theory and history. She is engaged in community participation through the use of the visual as a means to produce and interpret heritage. Wilkie has recently collaborated with Plot, an artist and writers collective, on the photographic artists' book *Brookhouse: Walking the Walls* (2011) and has spoken and written about her work in a number of settings, including presentations in Hungary, Portugal, Poland and the UK. She has contributed essays to a number of exhibition catalogues. Wilkie's chapter in *Recording Leisure Lives: Everyday Leisure in 20th Century Britain* (2012) links the work *Brookhouse* to Humphrey Spender's *Worktown* (1937-38) photographs for Mass Observation. In 2011 Wilkie convened the symposium *Photography & the Artist's Book* as part of the 6th Manchester Artists' Book Fair.

Theresa Wilkie is Director of Design & Culture and Senior Lecturer in Critical & Contextual Studies in the School of Art & Design, University of Salford, UK.

About the Contributors

Sarah Bodman is Senior Research Fellow for Artists' Books at the Centre for Fine Print Research (CFPR), at the University of the West of England, Bristol, UK, where she runs research projects investigating and promoting contemporary book arts. Sarah is also Programme Leader for the MA Multidisciplinary Printmaking course at UWE. She is the author of *Creating Artists' Books*, the editor of the *Artist's Book Yearbook* (a biennial reference publication on contemporary book arts), the *Book Arts Newsletter* and *The Blue Notebook* journal for artists' books. Sarah also writes a regular column on artists' books for the *ARLIS* News-Sheet, and the journal *Printmaking Today*. She has produced book works through etching, letterpress, pulp-printing, laser cutting, digital and video and is willing to use any process that best suits the work being made, from a typewriter to free download. Some recent works include *Cherry Blossom Island Tree* with Tom Sowden (unique book and video, 2009), *An Exercise for Kurt Johannessen* (free download, 2010), *No Dutch Details* with Tom Sowden (video bookwork, 2011), *TOAST: A Night on Weevil Lake* (collaborative bookwork and video for World Book Night, 2011), *An Inventory* (POD and ePub, for *An Inventory of al-Mutanabbi Street*, 2011) and *Do Not Enter* (unique pulp/screenprinted book, and ePub for Codex Event 8, 2012). http://www.bookarts.uwe.ac.uk

Sylvia Grace Borda is currently a Research Associate at Emily Carr University of Art and Design in Vancouver, Canada, and honorary Visual Arts Researcher at the University of Stirling. Sylvia has also held positions as the MA Convener for the Photography and Fine Art Program Queen's University Belfast, Senior Lecturer for Photography at the University of Salford, and as Associate Researcher in Visual and Digital Media at the University of British Columbia. Her research interests follow the development and convergence of early imaging, photography, optics, and the advent of alternative forms of visual communication. She has published and lectured on these topics as part of ISEA and CHART conferences, among others. As an artist and curator Sylvia has exhibited in North America, Europe and elsewhere. She has received a number of public grants and awards, including the Public Artwork Award recognition PWBC 2011 and Award of Excellence –ACEC 2012 for the City of Richmond, Canada Public Art Commission: No.4 Pump Station (2010-11); Cultural Capital of Canada Artist status award in combination with Cultural Olympiad project status for the Winter Olympics (2008-10); the Innovation Award, The Lighthouse Gallery Glasgow (2006), and the Urban Culture Award (through the Millennium Commission, Cities of Culture Liverpool) for 2005-07. Sylvia's work has been featured in *Photomonitor*, *UK Herald*, *Canadian Architecture*, *En Route Magazine – Air Canada*, *Architecture Today*, and *Editions Dazibao*.

Tim Daly studied photography at the Royal College of Art and has exhibited his documentary projects in national and international venues such as The Photographers' Gallery, London and NGBK, Berlin. Tim's research interest is in developing the photographic book as a primary form, where the locus of the piece resides in the book alone – where the reading of the work is influenced by physical interaction with materials presented in a non-codex form. He is currently Senior Lecturer in Photography at the University of Chester.

Lawrence George Giles is an award-winning visual artist with a strong record of exhibiting both nationally and internationally. His work engages with the field of oral and visual narrative and the use of the photograph as an *aide mémoire*. Specific interests have focused upon the panoramic format as a medium to extend both physical and temporal space as a means to investigate our relationship with time, memory and place. Additional interests have centred on issues relating to how digital art and media operate within specific artforms and the further exploration of how these media, once combined, can be exploited and developed within a digital platform. Lawrence is the programme leader of the BA (Hons) Photography programme at the University of Salford and is also co-founder and Vice Chair of *LOOK11*, Liverpool's first International Photography Festival.

Angela Kelly holds degrees in Creative Photography and Art Education and a Masters in Fine Art Photography. Originally from Belfast, Northern Ireland, Angela holds a tenured Associate Professor position at RIT, Rochester, NY where she has served as the coordinator of the MFA Imaging Arts Photography programme from 1994-99 and again from 2009-11. She was awarded a professional academic leave grant in 2011-12 to pursue her creative work. Collections holding her work include: the Center for Creative Photography,

Tucson, the Art Institute of Chicago, the Museum of Contemporary Photography, Chicago and the Arts Council, London. In 2011, she exhibited *Catharsis: Images of Post Conflict Belfast* at the 3rd International Photography Festival, Dali, China, where her exhibition was nominated out of 200 international exhibits for the best exhibit. *Catharsis* will be the subject of a forthcoming artist's book in 2013. www.AngelaKellyPhoto.com

Adam Murray is a lecturer and researcher in Photography at the University of Central Lancashire, and photographer and co-founder of *Preston is my Paris*. Adam's work focuses on subjects relating to everyday life and has been featured in a number of publications including *Photoworks*, *British Journal of Photography*, *Le Monde* and *The Blue Notebook: Journal for Artists' Books*. *Preston is my Paris* publications have been exhibited internationally and are held in the National Art Library at the Victoria & Albert Museum.

Elisabeth Neudörfl is Professor of Documentary Photography at Folkwang University in Essen, Germany. After vocational training as a photographer, she studied photography in

Dortmund at the University of Applied Sciences and Arts, and in Leipzig at the Academy of Visual Arts and has held teaching positions in Hanover and Leipzig. She has published her work in a number of photobooks: *E.D.S.A.* (2010) by Wiens Verlag; *Super Pussy Bangkok* (2006) by the Institut für Buchkunst Leipzig; *Future World* (2002) by the Sprengel Museum Hanover; *Plan* (1999, in collaboration with Bettina Lockemann) by the Institut für Buchkunst Leipzig. Solo exhibitions include *Habitat* (2010), Galerie Barbara Wien Wilma Lukatsch, Berlin; *Von der Straße* (2009), Galerie Barbara Wien, Berlin; *Future World* (2002), Sprengel Museum Hanover. Group exhibitions include *Photography Calling!* (2011/12), Sprengel Museum Hanover (Catalogue); *Ruhrblicke* (2010), Sanaa Building, Zeche Zollverein, Essen (Catalogue); *Hyper Cities/Über Städte* (2007), Museum of Asian Art, Berlin (Catalogue); *Towards a New Ease* (2007), Fotomuseum Winterthur, Switzerland and others in Pingyao (China), Dortmund, Stuttgart, Zagreb (Croatia) etc. In addition to private collections, her work is held in the collections of the Sprengel Museum Hanover and the Fotomuseum Winterthur. Elisabeth also writes about photography.

Jane Pendlebury has worked in the Sir Kenneth Green Library at Manchester Metropolitan University since 2000 and in MMU Special Collections since 2008. The Special Collections contain one of the most comprehensive collections of artists' books in the UK. Pendlebury works closely with this collection in terms of its accessibility and its ongoing development and spoke about this at the 2011 symposium *Photography & the Artist's Book*.

David Penny is a photographic artist and lecturer based in Manchester. Having studied photography at Manchester School of Art and the University of Westminster he is currently undertaking a Practice as Research PhD at MIRIAD, Manchester. In 2012 David will be exhibiting at the Open Eye Gallery, Liverpool; ShanghART Gallery, Shanghai; Sheffield Institute of the Arts and Curve Gallery, Newcastle, Australia. His work has previously been shown at Manchester Art Gallery, Bridewell Gallery - Liverpool, Wolstenholme Projects - Liverpool and Curve Gallery as part of the 2010 Liverpool Biennial. www.davidpenny.info

Jane Simon is a Lecturer in the Department of Media, Music, Communication and Cultural Studies at Macquarie University in Sydney, Australia. She researches and teaches across media studies, visual cultural studies and photography. Jane's approach to contemporary visual culture is also a practical one: she is a visual artist, specialising in photographic media and artists' books. Jane received her PhD in Gender and Cultural Studies at the University of Sydney in 2007. In 2010 she was awarded a Leverhulme Trust Visiting Fellowship to undertake research at the European Centre for Photographic Research at the University of Wales. She has published articles on amateur film, experimental film, photography, artist's books and modes of writing about visual culture in *Continuum: Journal of Media & Cultural Studies*, *M/C: A Journal of Media and Culture*, *Emotion Space & Society*, *Cultural Studies Review* and *The Blue Notebook: journal for artist's books*. Jane is currently working on a project that explores representations of domestic interiority in contemporary art photography.

Logan Sisley studied art history at the University of Otago and the University of Auckland, New Zealand. He is currently Exhibitions Curator at Dublin City Gallery The Hugh Lane, Ireland, and a member of the studio team for the studio 468 residency programme, Rialto, Dublin.

Diane Smyth is the deputy editor of the *British Journal of Photography*, and has also written on photography for *Aperture*, *PDN*, *Creative Review*, *Philosophy of Photography*, *Photomonitor*, *guardian.co.uk* and *thetimes.co.uk*. She has spoken on photography at The Photographers' Gallery, The Frontline Club, the Printed Matters Photobook Symposium and the London College of Communications, and reviewed portfolios at Format Festival, the National Media Museum, Rhubarb-Rhubarb and Photomonth.

Adam Paul Verity is a Senior Lecturer, and the Programme Leader of BA (Hons) Contemporary Lens Media, in the School of Art and Design, University of Lincoln, UK. He is a practising artist with a particular interest in the terrain between still and moving image. His current research interests include the personal photographic archive, the construction of visual narrative, and the artist's book. He has exhibited in the UK and internationally, and his work has featured in a number of photographic publications.

Index

Also from MuseumsEtc

Naturalistic Photography

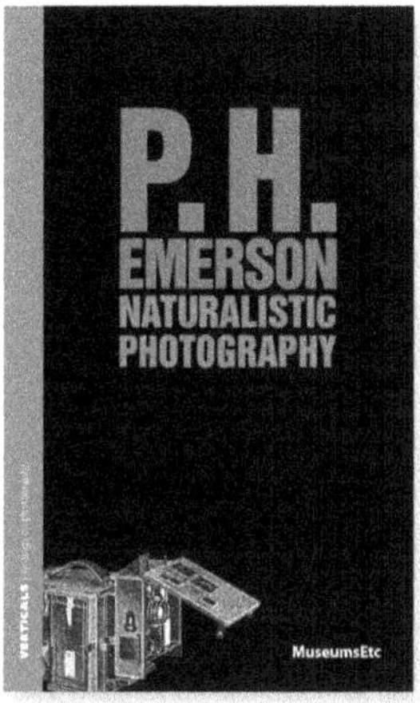

By P H Emerson

ISBN: 978-1-907697-58-6 [paperback]
ISBN: 978-1-907697-59-3 [hardback]

Order online
from www.museumsetc.com

P H Emerson's *Naturalistic Photography* is one of the classics of photographic literature.

This newly designed and typeset edition takes the text from the definitive 1899 edition and includes three additional essays by Emerson, among them the controversial *Photography - Not Art.*

Compared at the time to "dropping a bombshell at a tea party", *Naturalistic Photography* was the start of a crusade against the academism of artistic photography.

Dubbed "the Martin Luther of photography" (John Szarkowski), and more recently the "one of the most virulent polemicists in the history of photography" (Thomas Galifot, Musée d'Orsay), Emerson's fierce and trenchant writing is in sharp contrast to the gentle, atmospheric images of his pioneering photobooks *Life and Landscapes of the Norfolk Broads* and *Marsh Leaves.*

Emerson's texts are today recognised as ranking alongside those of John Berger, Roland Barthes and John Szarkowski, as the precursors to contemporary thinking on photography.

VERTICALS | writings on photography

History and Handbook of Photography
Gaston Tissandier (trans. John Thompson)

Naturalistic Photography
P H Emerson

Photography and the Artist's Book
Theresa Wilkie, Jonathan Carson & Rosie Miller (editors)

Photographic Studios of Europe
H Baden Pritchard

MuseumsEtc Books

Academic Museums: Exhibitions and Education
Academic Museums: Beyond Exhibitions and Education
Alive To Change: Successful Museum Retailing
Contemporary Collecting: Theory and Practice
Conversations with Visitors: Social Media and Museums
Creating Bonds: Successful Museum Marketing
Creativity and Technology: Social Media, Mobiles and Museums
Inspiring Action: Museums and Social Change
Interpretive Master Planning: Philosophy, Theory and Practice
Interpretive Master Planning: Strategies for the New Millennium
Interpretive Planning Handbook
Museum Retailing: A Handbook of Strategies for Success
Museums and the Disposals Debate
Museums At Play: Games, Interaction and Learning
Narratives of Community: Museums and Ethnicity
New Thinking: Rules for the (R)evolution of Museums
Restaurants, Catering and Facility Rentals: Maximizing Earned Income
Rethinking Learning: Museums and Young People
Science Exhibitions: Communication and Evaluation
Science Exhibitions: Curation and Design
Social Design in Museums: The Psychology of Visitor Studies (2 volumes)
Sustainable Museums: Strategies for the 21st Century
The New Museum Community: Audiences, Challenges, Benefits
The Power of the Object: Museums and World War II
Twitter for Museums: Strategies and Tactics for Success
Wonderful Things: Learning with Museum Objects

MuseumsEtc Videos

Cocktails and Culture: Cultivating Generation Next
Museums | Inclusion | Engagement
Planning and Designing for Children and Families
Real-World Twitter in Action

Order online at: www.museumsetc.com

Colophon

This edition first published in 2012
by MuseumsEtc Ltd
Hudson House
8 Albany Street
Edinburgh EH1 3QB

MuseumsEtc
675 Massachusetts Avenue
Suite 11
Cambridge
MA 02139

www.museumsetc.com

The paper used in printing this book comes
from responsibly managed forests and meets
the requirements of the Forest Stewardship Council™
(FSC®) and the Sustainable Forestry Initiative® (SFI®).
It is acid free and lignin free and meets all ANSI
standards for archival quality paper.

A CIP catalogue record for this book
is available from the British Library.

ISBN: 978-1-907697-50-0

Lightning Source UK Ltd.
Milton Keynes UK
UKHW022053301021
393098UK00006B/885

9 781907 697500